INSIGHT

LIS

Compact Guide: Lisbon is a culture-based guide for a culture-based destination, revealing the splendours of the city's monuments, the wealth of its museums, the atmosphere of its alleyways and the delights of its avenues and parks.

This is just one title in *Apa Publications'* new series of pocket-sized, easy-to-use guidebooks intended for the independent-minded traveller. Based on an award-winning formula pioneered in Germany, *Compact Guides* pride themselves on being authoritative and up-to-date. They are in essence mini travel encyclopedias, designed to be comprehensive yet portable, both readable and reliable.

Star Attractions

An instant reference to some of Lisbon's most popular tourist attractions to help you on your way.

Castello de São Jorge p22

Alfama p24

Igreja São Roque p29

Jerónimos Monastery p46

Tower of Belém p50

Museum of Ancient Art p53

Azulejos Museum p62

Sintra p66

Batalha p70

Convent of the Order of Christ p71

Sesimbra p73

LISBON

Introduction

Places

Culture

Leisure

Practical Information

Lisbon – City of Light and Shade

When the Swiss film maker Alain Tanner made his classic about the stranger wandering the streets and alleyways of Lisbon (1983), he called it *Dans La Ville Blanche* (In the White City). Many visitors before and after him have been struck by the quality of the light in Lisbon. The Atlantic seems to give the air a more subdued, softer appearance than the Mediterranean, even if that means sea fog occasionally rolling in off the ocean.

Despite those foggy days, in times past at least, Lisbon's gaze was always fixed firmly out to sea. Once a remote outpost of what was thought to be the farthest edge of the known world, by the 15th century the town had become the centre of Portugese exploration. It was from Lisbon that Vasco da Gama set out to India in 1498, on an expedition that broke the Venetian trading monopoly with the Orient and soon saw Portugal develop into a world power. It was from Lisbon that colonists set out to South America, Africa and the Far East, returning laden with riches that converted the town from a European backwater into a world city. Even after the catastrophic earthquake of 1755, no expense was spared in replanning and rebuilding. As Lisbon is one of the few capitals to have survived Europe's wars unscathed, many of the historic buildings remain intact, an enduring testimony to a prosperous and glorious past.

Lady selling corn, Baixa
Opposite: the Discoveries Monumen

But with so much light, there has to be a shadowy side. Over the last century, the city has grown too quickly, without proper planning. It sometimes grinds to a halt under the burden of traffic and on calm days the air is heavy with exhaust fumes, although it is hoped that the new extensions to the metro system will help alleviate this situation. Modern architecture has left many sores on the city's landscape. In the old town, there are areas which may strike the visitor as unspoilt and picturesque, but are in fact poor and decaying. As in all big cities, huge estates have sprung up, often lacking basic social amenities. In other parts of the city, there are shanty towns where the very poorest members of the community live in squalor. For most of this century, Lisbon has been at the centre of a shrinking and increasingly impoverished empire.

Shanty town

Yet it is the splendour of its historic past which contributes so much to the charm of this city. And its attractions do not simply lie in the wealth of the city's artistic treasures. To some extent it is possible for northern Europeans to see, smell, hear and feel how their own cities may once have looked and how the inhabitants lived their lives. Whatever may have been written in praise or condemnation of the city, there are few people who would willingly walk away from it.

The harbour

Inquisitive smiles

Location and Size

Lisbon owes its historical importance to its superb natural harbour, one of the most beautiful in the world. The city is set in an undulating landscape on the north bank of the Tejo (Tagus) river. The westernmost extremity of continental Europe, Cabo da Roca, is only 30km (20 miles) away.The city lies between the 38th and 40th parallel, the same latitude as Ibiza and the southern tip of Italy. Athens is the only European capital which is further south.

With a length of (1100km/700 miles), the Tejo is the longest river in the Iberian peninsula. About 40km (27 miles) before it flows into the Atlantic, it opens out into the Mar da Palha (Sea of Straw), which is 13km (8 miles) across at its broadest point narrowing down to an estuary only 2km (1½ miles) across before it disgorges into the ocean. The city centre lies at the eastern end of this narrow stretch of river about 15km (9 miles) inland. The city has grown from this point in both directions along the north bank of the river. The poorer parts of the city are near the dockyards, wharves and small industrial estates along the river. Since the turn of the century, Lisbon has expanded. It has spread not only along the banks of the Tejo but also to the north into the undulating hinterland, which, with its seven hills, is sometimes compared to Rome.

New Lisbon tower blocks

City layout

Since Portugal joined the European Community in 1986, the building boom has continued unabated and the shape of the city is changing rapidly. A visit to one of the city's many *miradouros* or a cruise on the river Tejo itself will provide a better picture of the whole conurbation. Lisbon's main areas are easily defined by the city's natural contours. The city centre, Baixa or lower town, lies on the small plain only a few metres above the level of the river. It was this area which was worst affected by the 1755 earthquake. In the aftermath of the disaster, the city was rebuilt in a symmetrical grid pattern. Looking down over Baixa, to the right as viewed from the river, stands the Castelo de São Jorge, a former fortress. Half way up the hill is the Sé, the city's cathedral, with the poor districts of Alfama and Mouraria lying at the foot. To the left of Baixa, is a second hill, Bairro Alto, also an old part of the city, but not seriously affected by the earthquake. The most important of Lisbon's roads is the Avenida da Liberdade, a wide street which gradually climbs up from Baixa to the Avenidas Novas, the new avenues built in the late 19th and early 20th century. To the west of the city centre lies Belém, the suburb which most vividly portrays the heyday of the Portuguese empire with its exquisite buildings, monuments and museums celebrating Portugal's maritime history.

Bairro Alto

A number of places offer a view across to the *outra banda*, the other bank: the Mar da Palha, the Lisnave docks or the viewing platform at Cristo Rei, the huge statue of Christ at the southern end of the 25 de Abril bridge.

The Cristo Rei statue

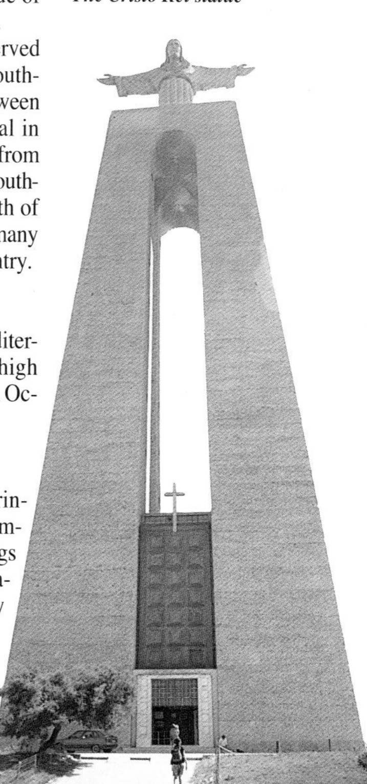

For many years, the wide estuary and river have served as a natural boundary. When the Arabs moved into southern Europe, the river represented the dividing line between Christians and Moslems and the region of Portugal in which Lisbon lies, the Estremadura, derives its name from this fact. At that time the region was at the 'extreme' southern end of Portugal. To this day, the land to the south of the Tejo, in Portuguese the *Alentejo*, is considered by many of Lisbon's inhabitants to be almost a different country.

Climate

Its proximity to the Atlantic gives Lisbon a mild, Mediterranean climate. It enjoys long, dry summers with high but not unbearable temperatures, and the period from October to March is mild but very wet.

Portugal's Capital City

As the capital of Portugal, Lisbon is home to the principal institutions of the republic. Many of the most important government offices are located in the buildings surrounding Commerce Square. The nation's parliament meets in the Palace of the National Assembly in the Bairro Alto, and in Belém the Royal Palace is now the official residence of the president of Portugal. The suburb of Belém, with its elegant buildings gives some insight into the role Lisbon once played at the hub of a worldwide empire. The 1960 Discoveries Monument with its museum dedicated to different aspects of the discoveries is also a demonstration of how the Portuguese were slow to adapt to changing times. It took Portugal much longer than Spain, Great Britain or France to come to the painful realisation that the era of colonial imperialism was ending. It was difficult for the nation to accept the loss of an empire because the illusion of imperial grandeur had become so firmly ingrained in the collective psyche.

Socialist Party symbol

Many Portuguese are inclined to criticise their country and its leaders when talking to foreigners, but this is misleading: they are expecting to be contradicted. These are difficult times. The country is performing an 180° turn, away from the Atlantic and beyond, and is now increasingly looking towards Europe for new partners. Even the old arch-rival, Spain, is seen in a new light and as a potential ally. Entry into the European Union has assisted the economic revival of the country and this will surely help to heal some of the deep scars. Be that as it may, even the post-1974 democratic governments have found it difficult to decentralise land administration. As ever, people from the provincial areas have to travel to Lisbon to resolve relatively minor issues. It is difficult for an outsider to imagine the chaos caused by a still largely centralised bureaucracy.

Political grafitti

Portugal has about 10 million inhabitants, but a further 3 million are obliged to work abroad, most of them in France. It is difficult to estimate how many of these migrant workers will return or will even want to do so. The district of Lisbon occupies only about 3 percent of Portugal's total area, but contains more than 20 percent of the population, a large proportion of whom are concentrated in the city itself.

The inland area of the country is very thinly populated and neglected, with the constant movement of people to the big cities of Oporto and to the Lisbon conurbation from Santarém to Setúbal continuing unchecked. A survey of young teachers who were asked where they would like to work showed that there were really only three options: Lisbon, Oporto and, to a much lesser extent, Coimbra, the university town in central Portugal.

Economy and Industry

The country is poor. The per capita gross national product is well behind that of Spain and it is at the bottom end of the European Union league table. The country cannot meet its own food requirements. Portugal has little in the way of mineral resources and only a few industries are well established. The flourishing tourist industry helps to offset the chronic trade deficit as do the (now rapidly diminishing) payments sent home by migrant workers, but unemployment still poses intractable problems, particularly for young people and for those in rural areas.

As far as industries are concerned, in Lisbon glass-making, electronics and diamond cutting have been added to the long-established local industries of soapmaking, munitions and steel. But the biggest development in recent years has taken place on the south bank of the Tajo, which has become the country's most important manufacturing centre. The port of Lisbon continues to expand, with moden facilities for container ships and car ferries.

Craftsmen's tools

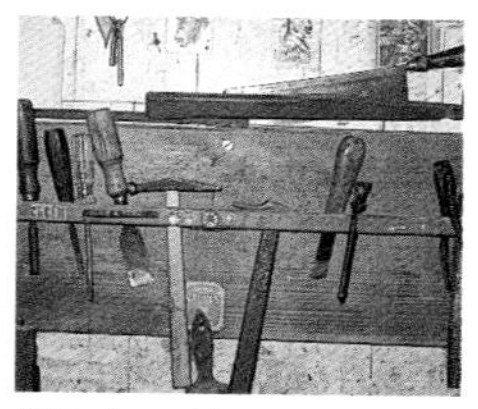

The Inhabitants of Lisbon

Lisbon's population within the city boundaries is reckoned to be 850,000, In the past 2,000 years, many different tribes and races have chosen to settle in Lisbon. The native Lusitanians were first subjected to an invasion by Celts, followed by the Romans who occupied the region for several centuries. Alans, Vandals and Visigoths sought to occupy the site, but only the latter tribe succeeded in winning control. The city later fell under Arabic rule and, despite many attempts to expel them, the Arabs maintained their hold on Portugal for hundreds of years. Finally, Portuguese colonial expansion brought Africans, Asians and South Americans to the city.

Elderly residents

If there are any characteristics which typify the racially-mixed Lisbon people, then they are politeness (except when at the wheel of a car), openness and a willingness to help strangers. Making conversation with the locals, in English or in French, ought not to be too difficult, but wearing scanty beachwear around the city centre is not the best way to win their approval.

Doing the laundry

Historical Highlights

It is likely that man had seen the potential of the sheltered, natural harbour in the Tejo estuary well before the Roman occupation (206BC). Clear evidence of earlier settlements have been found in the suburbs of the city. Baixa was covered by water at this time and two arms of the Tejo extended as far north as the present position of the Avenida da Liberdade and the Avenida do Almirante Reis. The Romans called their settlement Olisippo, as the earlier Phoenician traders had referred to Alis Ubbo meaning 'serene harbour'. Caesar made the town a *municipium* and named it *Felicitas Iulia*. Alans followed in the footsteps of the Romans but were ousted by the Visigoths who restored the original name of Ulixippona. They consolidated their position by making use of the Roman castle and securing the city walls, the remains of which can be seen in the Alfama district.

---

715 The Arab Moors sweep across the Iberian peninsula and take the city from the Visigoths. Arab culture penetrates all walks of life, bringing new agricultural techniques, including irrigation, as well as other new ideas such as shipbuilding, navigation, astronomy, mathematics and geography.

11TH CENTURY The Moslems are distracted by internal disputes and Christianity in northern Europe begins to spread south unimpeded.

1147 After a four-month siege, the future king Afonso Henriques, assisted by an army of Crusaders, succeeds in capturing Lisbon. Initially, Moslems are allowed to continue worshipping.

1173 St Vincent proclaimed Lisbon's patron saint.

1249 King Afonso III transfers Portugal's capital from Coimbra to Lisbon. The town grows rapidly: new walls are built to enclose what is now Baixa and also the area to the east of the Castelo.

1290 King Dinis founds a university, later moved to Coimbra.

1373 Anglo-Portugese Alliance signed, confirmed by 1386 Treaty of Windsor (unbroken to this day).

15TH CENTURY A new era begins for Portugal as the burgeoning middle-classes join forces with the king to agree on a grandiose plan for overseas expansion. The driving force is undoubtedly Prince Henry the Navigator (1394–1460), who, despite the name, takes no part in the great expeditions, but is responsible for training the crews, evaluating all known charts and records and improving the performance of the navigational instruments. As inheritors of the Arabs' maritime skills, the Portuguese have a start over their rivals.

Portuguese merchants are motivated by the profits to be made from the spice trade with the far east, and Vasco da Gama is not the only explorer to set off in search of a sea route to India. Untold riches pour into the city's coffers. In the 15th and 16th centuries, the town expands further and encompasses the hill on which Bairro Alto stands.

1500 Pedro Alvares Cabral lands in Brazil.

1578 Crisis over the succession in the Royal House of Avis. The 24-year-old King Sebastião embarks on a crusade against the Moors in Morocco and disappears, leaving no natural heir to the throne. The Spanish king, Felipe II, who has married Sebastião's sister, claims the Portuguese throne, as Filipe I of Portugal; the whole of the Iberian peninsula is now ruled from Madrid.

1580–1640 Period of Spanish domination. Lisbon loses influence and is regarded merely as a provincial capital. In 1581, the Spaniards decree that no foreign boats should enter Portuguese harbours, thus dealing a fatal blow to Portugal's merchants. When the Spanish armada is sunk in 1588, a large portion of the Portuguese navy is also lost. The booty from Portugal's colonies now no longer reaches Lisbon, but passes to Madrid.

---

1 DECEMBER 1640 A rebellion by Portuguese nobles ends Spanish rule and brings the House of Bragança to the throne. But the country's decline continues.

1703 Portugal and England sign the Methuen Treaty, a trade agreement dealing with wine exports and the import of manufactured goods. The agreement has disastrous consequences for Portugal as it only benefits a small group of aristocratic landowners and ruins the Portuguese woollen industry. Vast quantities of gold plundered from Brazil are frittered away without any real benefits to the economy.

1 NOVEMBER 1755 A catastrophic earthquake followed by tidal waves and fires hits Lisbon. A large part of the town is destroyed and about 30,000 of the 110,000 inhabitants perish. The Royal Palace is reduced to ruins, as is the building in Terreiro do Paço (Praça do Comércio) which housed all the colonial documents. Prime Minister Marquês de Pombal acts quickly to reconstruct the city. Pombal's insistence on the importance of trade gives a boost to the whole country.

1807–10 The British help Lisbon to escape assault by Napoleon's forces, but Britain demands costly trading privileges in return for this assistance.

1822 Brazil, under a Portuguese ruler, declares itself independent and Portugal, deprived of its gold supply, stumbles from one financial crisis to another. Until the middle of the 19th century a political struggle rages between the defenders of the authoritarian monarchy and the liberals who want to replace it with a constitutional monarchy.

1856 The first railway line opens in Lisbon, a project sponsored by foreign investors.

LATE-19TH CENTURY The first factories and new port installations are built along the banks of the Tejo between the city and Belém; more industrial centres later became established by the river on the eastern side of the city.

Following a series of colonial disputes with its oldest ally, Britain, Portugal suffers a crisis of confidence. Failure in the colonies undermines the authority of the crown, which suffers a loss of prestige. On top of the country's continuing financial problems, the workers begin to make demands.

1907 King Carlos I seeks to defuse the crisis by appointing a prime minister and granting him dictatorial powers. The following year, the king and his successor are assassinated on the Terreiro do Paço. Carlos's youngest son assumes power as Manuel II, but rules for only two years before seeking exile in Britain after a Republican revolution.

---

5 OCTOBER 1910 A republic is declared. But the government cannot solve the problems which led to the fall of the monarchy. Between 1910 and 1926, there are no less than 45 administrations.

1926 A military dictatorship is established, but its inability to come up with any effective solutions to the financial situation mean that chaos continues.

1928 Oliveira Salazar, an economist, becomes finance minister. He quickly balances the budget. He becomes prime minister in 1932 and proceesds to rule Portugal as a police state.

1939–45 Portugal remains neutral for the duration of World War II.

1961 The Salazar regime attempts to suppress the independence movements in the colonies, but this proves a drain on the nation's finances.

1968 Salazar cedes power to Marcelo Caetano on health grounds. Political opposition grows and illegal unions gain in strength, but the dictatorship manages to keep any rebellion under control.

EARLY 1970S Population pressure increases with migration from the countryside. Over 600,000 refugees from Portugal's newly independent colonies have to be absorbed during the 1970s and the government is confronted by serious housing shortage problems.

---

25 APRIL 1974 A song entitled *Grândola, Vila Morena* sung by a well-known political singer José Afonso is broadcast over the radio. This is the agreed signal to the Movimento das Forças Armadas for the start of the revolution. Mutinous troops seize control of the strategic points in the centre of Lisbon in accordance with a detailed plan prepared by an army major, Otelo de Carvalho. The old regime collapses as no serious attempt is made to defend it.

1986 Election of Social Democrat Mário Soares as the country's first civilian president in 50 years. Portugal joins the European Community and the transitional aid from the EC's coffers helps to create an economic boom

---

1987 and again in 1991, the centre-right under Prime Minister Cavaco Silva wins an absolute majority in elections.

SUMMER 1988 The Chiado district is seriously damaged by fire.

1991 Mario Soares re-elected president.

1994 Lisbon is the cultural capital of Europe.

VT. SIT. OM

TO.P.P.D.

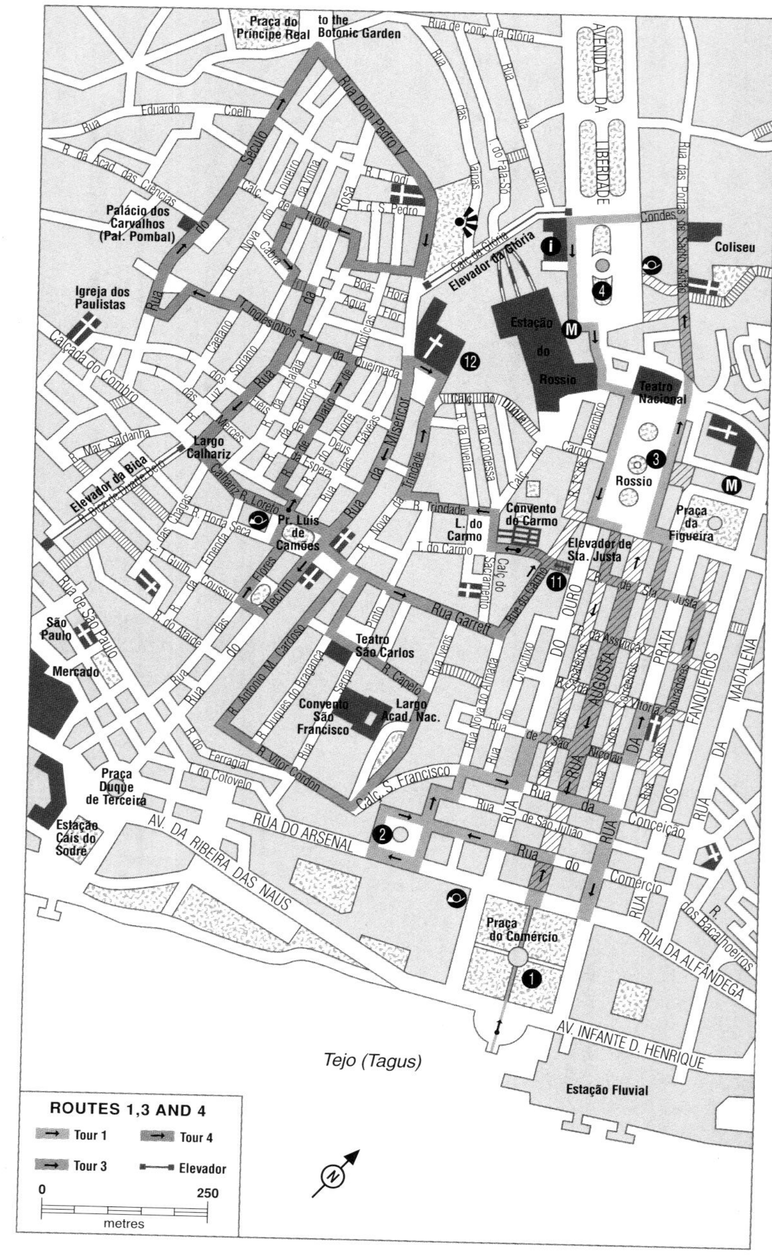
Praça do Príncipe Real
to the Botonic Garden
Rua de Conç. da Glória
AVENIDA DA LIBERDADE
Rua Dom Pedro V
Rua Eduardo Coelh
Século
R. da Acad. das Ciencias
Palácio dos Carvalhos (Pal. Pombal)
Igreja dos Paulistas
Calçada do Combro
Elevador da Glória
Calç. da Glória
Condes
Coliseu
Rua das Portas de Santo Antão
Estação do Rossio
Teatro Nacional
Rossio
Praça da Figueira
Largo Calhariz
Elevador da Bica
Pr. Luis de Camões
Rua da Misericor
Rua da Trindade
R. Trindade
L. do Carmo
Convento do Carmo
T. do Carmo
Elevador de Sta. Justa
Rua do Carmo
Rua Garrett
Teatro São Carlos
Convento São Francisco
Largo Acad. Nac.
R. Capelo
Rua Ivens
Rua Nova do Almada
Calç. S. Francisco
São Paulo
Mercado
Rua de São Paulo
Praça Duque de Terceira
Estação Cais do Sodre
AV. DA RIBEIRA DAS NAUS
RUA DO ARSENAL
Rua do Comércio
Rua da Conceição
Rua de São Julião
RUA DO OURO
RUA AUGUSTA
RUA DA PRATA
RUA DOS FANQUEIROS
RUA DA MADALENA
Praça do Comércio
RUA DA ALFÂNDEGA
AV. INFANTE D. HENRIQUE
Estação Fluvial
Tejo (Tagus)
ROUTES 1,3 AND 4
Tour 1
Tour 4
Tour 3
Elevador
0
250
metres

Trams in the square
Preceding pages, Praça do Comércio

Route 1

Baixa

This route covers the part of the city which was destroyed by the 1755 earthquake. It was completely rebuilt in the years that followed. Baixa should be visited during the daytime, when it is at its most lively. There is plenty od opportunity for window shopping on the way.

The devastation of Lisbon's city centre in 1755 gave the authorities an opportunity to start afresh, to redesign a city centre from nothing. Marquês de Pombal ordered the city's top architects and town-planners to prepare plans. One plan suggested rebuilding the old streets and recreating the past, another proposed that the ruins be left standing and that the heart of the new city centre be moved westwards towards Belém. But Pombal decided in favour of a layout which can still be seen today: a large square by the bank of the river on the site of the old royal palace; a rectangular grid of wide streets and a second square, the Rossio, away from the river to the north of the ruined quarter. Both squares adjoin the grid at right angles, thereby retaining a neat, geometrical balance.

Praça do Comércio arcades

The buildings themselves were also to follow a unified pattern. Originally all the houses were to be two storeys – the horror of the earthquake was still fresh in people's minds – but the land in the heart of the city was regarded as too valuable for low-rise structures. Engineers came up with a specially-designed wooden skeleton which was reckoned to be strong enough to support five storeys. But a characteristic feature of Pombal's Baixa was the attention to detail, such as the stylised designs on the window surrounds. Unfortunately, not all of Pombal's buildings have survived, so the sense of architectural unity is lost amid the many more recent structures.

Three architects worked on rebuilding Baixa: 80-year-old Manuel de Maia, Eugénios dos Santos, who died in 1760 and the Hungarian Carlos Mardel. Many examples of Mardel's work can still be seen around Lisbon. He worked, for example, with Maia on the construction of the huge aqueduct (*see page 57*).

To get the tour off to a grand start, take a boat trip from the landing stage at the eastern corner of the ★ **Praça do Comércio** ❶, or Terreiro do Paço as the local people still call it. Boats leave at regular intervals to Cacilhas on the southern bank of the Tejo and it has to be admitted that there is little of interest there, but the return journey gives passengers the view of the city that the many famous Portuguese seafarers enjoyed. On the right, towering above the city, is the former fortress, the Castelo de São Jorge, and clearly visible towards the bottom of the hill is the cathedral. To the left are the Bica and Bairro Alto, hilly quarters covered with huddles of old houses. The huge gateway in Praça do Comércio marks the entrance to Baixa, on a plain between the two hills. This panorama is probably the finest in Lisbon.

King José I

The Praça itself is an almost perfect square. The unified arcaded buildings which surround it are pure Pombal. They house many different government offices – on the left is the post office. The monument in the middle is an equestrian statue of King José I, who is mainly remembered for relinquishing power to his prime minister, Pombal, who was then free to set about the task of rebuilding the city unhindered. He is immortalised in a bronze medallion on the pedestal of the statue.

The gateway to Rua Augusta is a triumphal arch which dates from 1873, but was envisaged in the original plans. Through the arch, turn left along Rua do Comércio to a second, smaller square, the **Praça do Município** ❷. The **ornate pillars** in the centre fulfilled two functions: they served as a pillory *(pelourinho)* where wrong-doers were exposed to public abuse, and as a symbol of the town's jurisdiction. The square is dominated by the Câmara Municipal, the town hall. Completed in 1875, 100 years after the *pelourinho*, its neoclassical exterior contrasts with the ostentatious interior. The small chapel to the left of the town hall dates from 1810 and was dedicated to São Julião. Diagonally opposite is an attractive art nouveau facade dating from 1917.

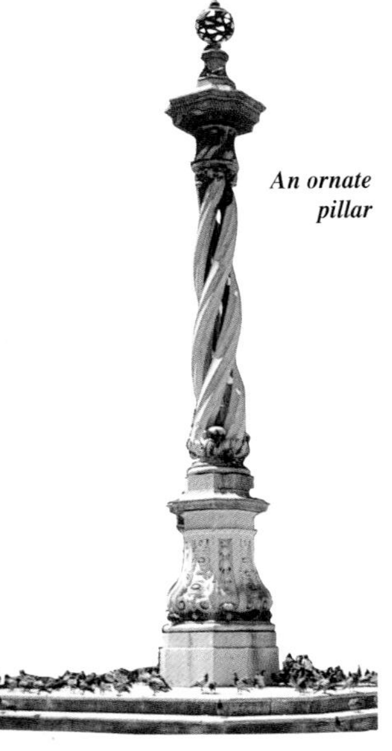

An ornate pillar

Turn left into Rua do São Julião and look for the 1919 banking house, a heavily-ornamented building on the left-hand side of the road. This part of Baixa, lying close to the river, has always been the banking quarter. An even grander bank is located in Rua do Ouro (Street of Gold), a little further along this walk. It was built at numbers 82–92 in 1905 for the Totta & Açores Bank.

A bank is obviously the right sort of building for the 'Street of Gold', but originally the streets were named after the different trades, which were usually clustered together in the same areas. Rua do Ouro, or sometimes Rua Áurea was the goldsmiths' street, Rua da Prata was for silversmiths, Rua dos Sapateiros, for shoemakers and Rua dos Douradores, for gold-platers.

Take Rua do São Nicolau across Baixa from west to east. The church of São Nicolau, with its facade of *azulejos*, was built and improved between 1780 and 1850. Turn left into Rua dos Douradores, which displays none of the elegance of the other main north–south roads, the shops are less grand and tradesmen live and work here. Turning into Rua da Santa Justa, the curious iron, neo-Gothic tower of Elevador de Santa Justa (*see page 28*) looks down over the shoppers. Renovation work on the lift was completed in 1994.

Rua dos Correeiros cuts through to the end of Baixa and leads into the two city centre squares, Praça da Figueira and the Rossio. Before the earthquake, a large hospital stood on the site of the Praça da Figueira. It then became the market-place, but the old covered market was pulled down in 1953. If time is available, it is interesting to glance inside the old shops bordering this square to admire their beautiful interiors. There is also a view of the Castelo de São Jorge from here.

Praça da Figueira, with its bronze statue commemorating the first king of the House of Avis, João I, is generally quieter than the bustling **Rossio**, ❸ or Praça de Dom Pedro IV as it is sometimes known. A marble pillar topped with a statue of Pedro IV dominates the square. Dom Pedro IV renounced the Portuguese throne to become the emperor of Brazil in 1822. The Rossio was earlier the place where heretics were burnt and later, in the 19th century, bullfights were staged here. Nowadays, there is generally less excitement, as *lisboetas* sit and watch the world go by from the comfort of the popular cafés. The Pastelaria Suiça is a favourite meeting place. The Rossio is spoilt, however, by traffic fumes and noise, as it is a notorious bottleneck. Rossio is the southern terminus of the Metro, although this may one day be extended as far as the river. It is a part of Lisbon which is never quiet. Lottery ticket sellers, shoeshiners and street traders, even sometimes the Salvation Army, can cause just as much congestion as the traffic.

The classical **Teatro Nacional Dona Maria II** stands on the northern side of the square. Built in 1846, it was destroyed by fire in 1964 and left in ruins for several years. The figure of Gil Vicente, the founder of Portuguese theatre, can be seen above the portico. On the right-hand side behind the theatre is the former palace of the Counts of

Totta and Açores Bank

Praça da Figueira

Café life in Rossio Square

Almada. It was started in 1509 and has been altered many times, but it is now the centre for the Association of Disabled Ex-Servicemen. Many soldiers were injured in Portugal's colonial wars during the 1960s and 1970s.

Continue along the lively Rua des Portas de Santo Antão with displays outside many of the food stores. The tasty but expensive seafood always looks very tempting. In the 15th century, the town wall was situated nearby and the street derives its name from one of the gates. There are some interesting buildings to look out for: the Casa do Alentejo (No 58) dates from the 17th century but was extensively rebuilt in 1918 with *azulejos* and Moorish-style extras. Every district of Lisbon had a house similar to this one during the Salazar regime; often it was just a meeting-place for 'provincials' who had settled there. A little further, again on the right-hand side, is the Coliseu, a huge 19th-century hall, which was a centre for political rallies as well as for concerts, ranging from classical music to variety shows. The auditorium, the largest in the city, can accommodate 7,000 people. The huge glass dome was constructed in Berlin.

Tempting seafood

Monument in Praça dos Restauradores

The Elevador da Glória

The Chamber of Commerce, directly opposite at numbers 87–91 was originally a cinema. The Politeama, two houses further, is now a cinema: opened in 1913 as a theatre, it has seen better times. The last of the cinemas is the Odeon. The tiny Rua dos Condes on the left cuts through to **Praça dos Restauradores** ❹. The name of this square derives from the restoration of Portuguese independence after 60 years of Spanish rule. From the north of the square, Avenida da Liberdade climbs gently upwards. Intended as a prestigious thoroughfare leading into the heart of the city, this boulevard was laid out at the end of the 19th century. For the energetic, a stroll up the hill will reveal a mix of architectural styles, ranging from some of the original, imposing town houses to plain and inappropriate new blocks. At the upper end of Avenida da Liberdade, this route links with Route 5 (*see page 37*).

The building which houses the tourist information centre on the west side of Praça dos Restauradores is the Palácio Foz. Begun in 1755 in rococo style, it was completed in the 19th century in classical style. Just to the right is the funicular railway, the **Elevador da Glória**, which leads up to Bairro Alto (*Routes 3 and 4*). The Eden cinema to the left of the palace dates from the 1930s. The cinema was until recently very popular among working people, but the video boom has taken its toll on cinema attendances here too. Return to the Rossio, but notice the Hotel Avenida Palace, another impressive example of the architectural style popular at the end of the 19th century. It is difficult to believe, but the **station** nearby (Estação da Rossio) was designed by the same architect, J. Luis Monteiro. Built in 1887, it is one of the few remaining examples of neo-Manueline architecture. Originally it was the station for international trains, but the ground floor is now a shopping centre, while the first floor is used by suburban trains to Sintra and the west coast. On the opposite side of the road, a booking office for concert and theatre tickets, etc is situated in an ornate pavilion dating from the end of the last century.

On the west side of the Rossio is the **Café Nicola** (No 25), one of Lisbon's most popular cafés. In earlier times, it was the meeting-place of a coffee-house literary circle, where writers and journalists sought inspiration. Take a look at the ornate interior of the Tabacaria Mónaco (No 21). At the southern end of the Rossio, a small arch marks the start of Rua dos Sapateiros and on the right-hand side is Lisbon's first **cinema**, built in art nouveau style in 1907. Rua dos Sapateiros is one of the quieter, gloomier streets in Baixa and a good place to draw breath after the hectic Rossio. Cut through Rua de Santa Justa to Rua Augusta. Now pedestrianised, it is popular with street traders and pavement artists.

Before returning to the triumphal arch in Praça do Comércio, make a detour along Rua da Conceição to Rua da Prata. On the corner at numbers 61–63 is the delightful Vianna tea and coffee shop, more or less unchanged since the middle of the 19th century. And on the left-hand side, hidden under the arcades of Praça do Comércio, is the **Martinho da Arcada**, Lisbon's oldest café and an ideal place for a well-earned drink. Fernando Pessoa, Portugal's most respected 20th-century poet, used to be a regular customer here.

The station

Art nouveau cinema detail

The Café Nicola

Route 2

★ Cathedral – ★★ Castelo de São Jorge – ★★ Alfama – ★ Graça – Mouraria.

Santa Madalena church

This route covers the oldest quarters of the city and an area which was little affected by the 1755 earthquake. Several hours will be required, but the walk can easily be split up into two sections, by starting the route as described but taking a tram back to Baixa at the church of São Vicente de Fora. For the second part, take the tram to Largo das Portas do Sol and restart the walk. It is possible to take in a small tour of the Graça quarter from São Vicente as well (*see page 27*).

Take Rua da Prata from the northeastern corner of Praça do Comércio ❶, then follow Rua do Comércio and Rua da Madalena to the **church of Santa Madalena**. Built in 1783, it retains a Manueline porch from an earlier church. Below and to the west of the cathedral is the lovely baroque church of Santo António da Sé, dedicated to St Anthony, Lisbon's patron saint, whose festival is cele-

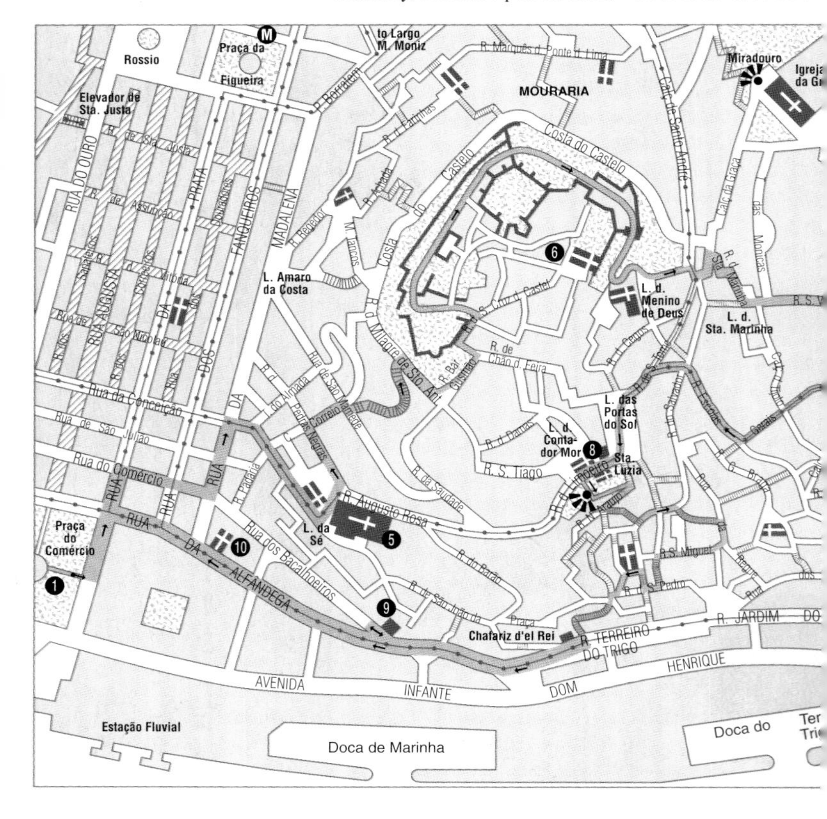

brated on 13 June. The present church dates from 1767. It is said that the crypt, which was part of an earlier church was built exactly where St Anthony of Padua, the son of a noble, was born in 1185. The newer sacristy is decorated with flower-patterned *azulejos*. The visit of Pope John Paul II to celebrate the 750th anniversary of St Anthony's death is recorded on a tiled picture in the crypt. St Anthony is remembered for his sermons and also as the patron saint of the forgetful.

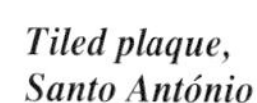

Tiled plaque, Santo António

We now come to the ★ **Cathedral** ❺. The bishop's seat is often referred to as the Sé (from the Portuguese word *sede* meaning seat). Lisbon's Sé is the oldest maintained building in the city. It is thought to have been built in the 12th century shortly after the city was recaptured from the Moors, and stands on the site of their mosque. Some of the stones from the mosque were used in its construction as well as a Visigothic frieze dating from before Arab rule, which had apparently been damaged by gases emitted during the destruction of the mosque, but which has now been restored. The frieze is on view in the cloister to the left of the entrance. From the outside, the church looks to be pure Romanesque, but this unity of style comes as a result of frequent restorations and alterations after the many earthquakes.

Vaulting detail in the cathedral

The interior, however, does show many different styles. The nave and aisles were restored in Romanesque, but the choir and organs are baroque, as is the large crib in the north aisle, which is the work of the sculptor Machado de Castro. The chapels in the ambulatory are typically Gothic. Look specially for the 14th-century **tombs of Fernandes Pacheco** and his wife in the third chapel on the right. A faithful stone dog watches over the long sleep of his master. The cloister can be reached via the ambulatory and at a lower level has late Romanesque/early Gothic features. A particularly

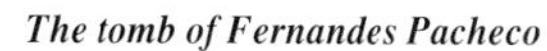

The tomb of Fernandes Pacheco

Castelo de São Jorge

impressive wrought-iron screen is worth investigating. None of the many treasures in the sacristy are of any special significance.

The walk to the castle avoids the usual route and follows a quieter path. Take Rua das Pedras Negras to Calçada do Corrieo Velho, or the old post office, a grand, 18th-century mansion painted in red but covered in scaffolding at the time of going to press. The climb starts with the Escadas do São Crispim (St Crispin's stairway). This slightly unusual passage consists of an assortment of buildings dating from before Pombal's time. From the top take a close look at the house opposite. The date above the door shows the year of construction and then there is a fine ornamented pavilion up to the left in the small garden.

Turn right, then left to ★ **Castelo de São Jorge** ❻. The Romans built a castle on top of this hill, which later fell to the Arabs, but when the Portuguese retook the city, it became the king's residence. The castle walls were damaged in the earthquake of 1755 and it was not fully restored until the 20th century during the Salazar regime. During the restoration, more attention was paid to retelling the history of the nation than creating a faithful reconstruction. Nevertheless, it offers a fine ★★ **view** of the city, the river and beyond. *Azulejo* pictures dating from 1963 point out the main landmarks and it should be remembered that at that time the Tejo bridge had not been built nor had most of the high-rise blocks. A small park with water courses and animal enclosures has been laid out within the courtyard of the castle ruins. By following the walls round, Graça's church and beneath that the old quarter of Mouraria (*see page 27*) come into view. The north-east-

Castle opening times

View from the castle

ern Santo André gate is the only entrance. The castle is open from 9am to 7pm, but during the summer months stays open until 9pm.

In Largo de Menino Deus, at number 4, stands a fine 16th-century house, which survived the ravages of the earthquake. The ★ **Igreja do Menino Deus** also predates the earthquake, but it suffered some damage. Like many of Lisbon's buildings, it was never fully restored and the towers have not been replaced. If by good fortune the church is open, then the **interior** is worth more than just a cursory glance. It is richly decorated but not overdone, with white and painted marble around the octagonal nave giving an airy feeling to an otherwise restricted space. If the church is not open, loud and persistent knocking at the adjoining entrance door may attract the attention of the resident keyholder.

Cross Largo Rodrigues de Freitas and Rua da Santa Marinha to the ★ **São Vicente de Fora** ❼, once outside (in Portuguese: *de fora*) the town walls. Although not situated on top of a hill, like the Basílica da Estrela in the west, it is a landmark which can be easily located whether from the castle or the river.

The church in its present form was commissioned by Filipe II, one of three Spanish regents. Designed by the Italian architect Filippo Terzi, it was completed in 1629 and could be described as Mannerist or early baroque in style. The strongly symmetrical facade contrasts with the baroque **interior**, part of which has been extensively modified. The organ and Machado de Castro's high altar with baldachin are particularly striking. Six small side chapels, three on each side, help to counter the vastness of the long nave.

Enter the former Augustinian monastery from the right-hand side of the nave. The baroque 18th-century *azulejo* pictures in the entrance hall tell the story of the monastery and also the heroic deeds of Afonso Henriques in his battles of Santarém and Lisbon (*see page 10*). In one of the two cloisters the fables of La Fontaine are depicted. Sadly, many of the tiles are now in a poor condition; at the time of going to press the complex was closed for renovation. Ask at the tourist office for up-to-date information.

On Tuesday and Saturday, the long-established Feira da Ladra or **Thieves' Market** is held behind the church on the Campo de Santa Clara. There is generally little of interest to find there and, although highly regarded by some, is generally reckoned to have deteriorated as traders see tourists as their best customers.

For a detour into the Graça quarter, *see page 27*.

Head downhill from São Vicente by Calçada de São Vicente and then follow Rua das Escolas Gerias, a tram route with some tortuous bends, as far as Largo das Portas do

Interior detail, Igreja do Menino Deus

Plaque depicting St Vincent

Interior of São Vicente

Miradouro de Santa Luzia

Sol, where the **Palácio Azurara** ❽, a handsome 17th-century palace, houses the Museu de Arte Decorativas (Museum of Decorative Art). Many of the exhibits were donated by wealthy citizens and they show the development of furniture. Bedrooms, dining rooms, function rooms and music rooms from different periods of Portuguese history are tastefully displayed. The museum is also a training workshop for craft workers (Tuesday to Saturday 10am–1pm, 2.30–5pm). At the time of going to press, the building was closed for renovation.

Directly opposite the palace is the **Miradouro de Santa Luzia**, which offers a fine panorama over Lisbon. There are many viewing points in the city and Santa Luzia may not be the best, but it is certainly a good spot to take a break, with its carefully cultivated garden and the large *azulejo* panel which depicts the Terreiro de Paço before the earthquake.

A few yards back from the *miradouro* are the steps down to what is probably the most famous part of the city, ★★ **Alfama.** It survived the earthquake virtually unscathed and the maze of narrow streets, alleys and staircases has remained unchanged since the Arab occupation. No houses remain from that era and there are few buildings of special note. Its appeal rests rather in its unique atmosphere. As a major tourist attraction, Alfama also draws pickpockets and thieves. Visitors should take every precaution with handbags and cameras.

A street in Alfama

It is easy to feel part of a different world here. Vehicular access to the narrow streets is almost impossible, making Alfama perhaps the original pedestrian precinct. The predominant smells are not of exhaust fumes but of musty houses and poor sewers, but at lunchtimes and evenings, more appetising smells waft through the street as the local people grill fish on primitive barbecues by the front doors. Fishwives call out noisily as they walk the narrow streets, with fish for sale in large baskets balanced on their heads.

A street barbecue

It is picturesque but poor. The houses are packed tightly together and everyone seems to know everyone else. The tourists who take over the quarter by day and then throng the streets again at night in search of *fado* music, are generally treated with indifference by the locals. To the surprise of many, Alfama has managed to resist the tourist onslaught and has retained much of its original character.

The labyrinth of streets is not easy to navigate even with a map. It is much more fun simply to wander along the winding alleyways and explore the nooks and crannies, and it is quite difficult to get lost in this relatively compact district. Having arrived in Alfama from the steps leading down from the Santa Luzia *miradouro*, keep turning left through a number of narrow streets as far as Rua de

Regueira. This street finally widens into a small square and a glance up the Beco do Carneiro will reveal an alleyway so narrow that there is barely room for two people to pass.

Turn right here along Rua do São Miguel, at the far end of which stands the church of São Miguel, consecrated in 1775. It is worth pausing to admire its baroque interior, but again, finding someone with a key can sometimes be a problem. Several alleys link Rua do São Miguel with Rua de São Pedro, which is a little further south and is Alfama's main shopping street.

Across Largo de São Rafael is the Judiaria, an old Jewish ghetto. Rua da Judiaria follows the course of the old Visigothic-Moorish town wall, of which some parts are still visible. An archway leads out of Alfama and into **Largo do Terreiro do Trigo.** The name means corn square, as it was here that the town's grain was stored, once it had arrived at the port. Just on the right around the corner is the oldest fountain in the city, the **Chafariz d'el Rei**. It is not clear which king *(rei)* was responsible for building the original fountain, but it must have placed heavy demands on the local water supply, particularly as the ships moored nearby also needed to have their tanks replenished for the voyage ahead before weighing anchor. Inevitably, access to the limited water supplies led to arguments and fights, before a ruling by the municipal authorities in 1551 decreed who could draw water from the six available pumps. The present fountain was constructed in 1747, in front of the town walls, but a handsome 19th-century villa now forms the backdrop.

Follow the road back to the city centre. A few customs sheds remain here from the days when this section of the

Resident and tradesman of Alfama

Detail of the Chafariz d'el Rei

Casa dos Bicos

river was a busy harbour and warehouse centre. In Rua dos Bacalhoeiros (Cod Fishermen's Street) is the ★ **Casa dos Bicos** ❾, or the House of Facets, which has an extraordinary facade of pyramid-shaped, pointed stones. It was commissioned in 1523 by Brás de Albuquerque, the illegitimate son of the first viceroy of India and President of Lisbon's Senate.

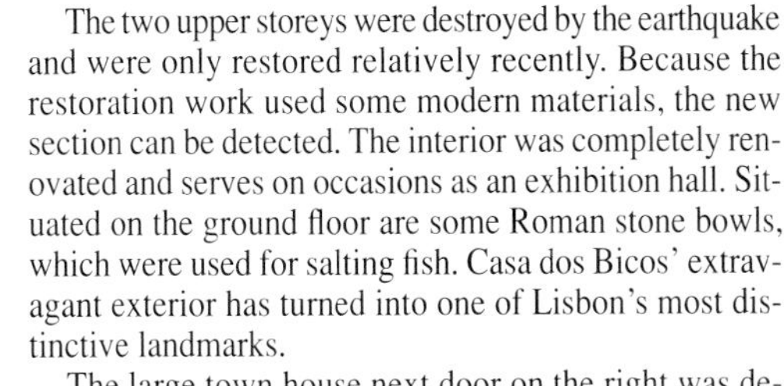

The two upper storeys were destroyed by the earthquake and were only restored relatively recently. Because the restoration work used some modern materials, the new section can be detected. The interior was completely renovated and serves on occasions as an exhibition hall. Situated on the ground floor are some Roman stone bowls, which were used for salting fish. Casa dos Bicos' extravagant exterior has turned into one of Lisbon's most distinctive landmarks.

Igreja da Conçeicão Velha

The large town house next door on the right was designed in 1755 by the architect Carlos Mardel and is typical of the Pombal era – apart from the upper storeys with balconies which were added later. A brick-built gabled house opposite has a north European feel and was built at the beginning of this century as a warehouse.

Follow Rua da Alfândega to reach the **Igreja da Conçeicão Velha** ❿, with its magnificent Manueline porch. This porch, like the two windows, were saved from the Igreja da Misericórdia, which was damaged beyond repair by the earthquake. King Manuel and his sister Leonor are depicted above the door but under the protective mantle of the Madonna.

A few yards further along Rua da Alfândega is Praça do Comércio, the finishing point of this route.

Detour into the ★ Graça quarter

A tour of the Graça quarter is a worthwhile detour for those who have time to spare. The area is interesting for its 19th-century architecture and can be reached either by a **28 tram** or from São Vicente de Fora along Rua Voz do Operário (The Voice of the Worker). This street derives its name from a workers' association which was founded at the end of the 19th century as a self-help group. Rua Voz do Operário eventually opens on to Largo da Graça. Turn left at the square to reach the **Igreja da Graça**. This church has an interesting 17th-century *azulejo* altar frontal, with warm tones creating the effect of brocaded textiles – a style known as *tapetes*, or carpets.This is another point in the city which offers a fine panorama.

The 28 tram in Graça

Graça is a working-class quarter which grew up at the turn of the century. One interesting example of workers' cottages is Villa Sousa, which can be seen through the entrance to number 82, opposite the church. But the best example is Villa Berta in Rua do Sol à Graça (55-59), where the houses are fronted by tiny gardens. Rua do Sol à Graça is the first street on the right at the pointed end of Largo da Graça. Follow the tram lines in Rua da Graça as far as Rua Virginia in the Estrela do Ouro settlement. The **pavements** on the estate are decorated with star patterns which give the area its name – *estrela* is Portugese for star. The houses are neat, but pause for a minute and count the doors to get some idea of how many families share a relatively small space.

Star-patterned pavement

To return to the city centre without using the main routes, cross the crescent of red houses at the end of Rua São Gens and turn right. Calçada do Monte leads down into the **Mouraria** quarter – another district whose origins date from the Arab occupation but one that is not so well known as Alfama. In fact, it became a refuge for the Arab community after the city was taken by the Christians. As it was outside the city walls, it was regarded as suitable for non-believers. The quarter has a certain charm, although it is now so badly run-down that newspapers frequently carry reports of buildings which are in danger of collapsing. On the other hand, unlike Alfama, there is not a so-called 'typical' *fado* restaurant on every other corner. Descend through the maze of alleys to emerge somewhere near Largo Martim Moniz, a notorious bottleneck, which is in desperate need of improvement. It is only a short walk from here back to Praça da Figueira and then the Rossio Square (*see Route 1, page 17*).

Like the Alfama district, Graça and Mouraria are great places to enjoy the festivities on 12 June, the eve of St Antony's day, when they host huge street parties.

The Convento do Carmo

Museum exhibit

Route 3

Trindade – Chiado (*see map on page 14*)

Route 3 will take rather less time than Route 2. It covers the area hit by the fire in the summer of 1988 and it begins at the lift ★ **Elevador de Santa Justa** ⓫ or as it is sometimes described, the Elevador do Carmo. This extremely novel, but practical means of public transport was designed by the French engineer Mesnier du Ponsard and was built between 1898 and 1901. The tower is an iron construction, ornamented in neo-Gothic style with traces of filigree and from the top there is a splendid panoramic ★ **view** of the city. The full extent of the fire can also be appreciated, although fortunately the flames were extinguished only a matter of yards from the lift itself. Extensive restoration work on the lift was completed in 1994.

A bridge leads from the top of the tower into Rua do Carmo, from where the ruined ★ **Convento do Carmo** can be seen on the right. This former Carmelite monastery was never rebuilt after the earthquake. Nuno Álvares Pereira vowed that if he defeated Castile at the Battle of Aljubarrota (1385) and secured Portugal's independence, he would build a church. Work on the church and convent started in 1389 and its founder spent the last years of his life there.

The ruined Gothic church with its elegant arched portal is now an **archaeological museum**. It possesses a special atmosphere as some of the exhibits are displayed in a roofless part of the ruins. The museum contains a finely ornamented marble pillar, which was found in Baixa and is believed to date from the time of the Visigoths. The museum is also occasionally used for open-air concerts. Opening times: 10am–1pm and 2–5pm, in summer 10am–5pm. Closed Saturday and holidays.

The view from the Elevador de Santa Justa

The headquarters of the Guarda Nacional Republicana, the Portuguese riot police, are housed in the nearby monastery. On 25 April 1974, the monastery witnessed some dramatic scenes as Marcelo Caetano, Salazar's successor, sought refuge in the barracks from the revolutionary troops. When they threatened to storm the building, he gave himself up and was taken to the airport in a tank. In the middle of the quiet Largo do Carmo stands an attractive, stone fountain, which was built in 1876. The silvery blue kiosk dates from the end of the 19th century.

There used to be a second large monastery nearby which was dedicated to the Holy Trinity and the district became known as Trindade. On the right side of Rua da Trindade at numbers 28–32 stands a house dating from the second half of the 19th century with a splendid display of *azulejos*. The artist Luís Ferreira has included some freemasonry symbols on the tiles. The nearby large red building is the Teatro de Trindade.

To the right, round the corner in Rua Nova Trindade, is the **Cervejaria da Trindade**, a beer hall which was established in the refectory of the old Trindade monastery. It is not just a place to enjoy good beers, but also somewhere to go for a cheap meal with seafood a speciality. In the summer, the big room can be pleasantly refreshing and cool, although there may be space in the garden. But even someone who is neither hungry nor thirsty, should take a look inside and admire the *azulejos* in the first hall, again the work of Luís Ferreira from 1863. The tiles depict the four seasons and various allegorical tales.

A little bit further on in Praça Trindade Coelho are two old kiosks, and also the ★★ **Igreja São Roque ⓬**, which, like São Vicente de Fora, was built according to designs by the Italian Terzi. The flat, largely undecorated facade conceals unimaginable treasure. Although the facade had to be rebuilt after the earthquake, the interior was more or less undamaged. The church takes its name from the São Roque chapel which is thought to have stood on the original site.

São Roque was commissioned by the Jesuits at the end of the 16th century and characterises the architecture of the Counter-Reformation. The Mannerist style, which followed the Renaissance and which is epitomised in São Roque, was for a time known as the Jesuit style, so influential were these counter-reformationists in the realm of ecclesiastical architecture. Typical of the period is the single-naved interior, which is relieved only by the decorations of the side chapels. The worshippers were expected to give their undivided attention to the service and the sermon and not be otherwise distracted. Side aisles were abandoned to improve the acoustics, but equally typical is the 'horror vacui', a fear of emptiness, which led

A member of the Guarda

Cervejaria da Trindade

Plaque on São Roque

the artists to ensure that no part of the church went undecorated. The oldest *azulejos* can be seen in the ★ third chapel from the entrance, which is dedicated to São Roque. The tiles on the left side wall are the work of the artist Francisco de Matos and the clearly visible date 1584 denotes their year of manufacture. The murals in this chapel are of a remarkable size for that period and they must have required very detailed planning. The central picture on the right-hand side which shows the saint healing a plague-sufferer has well-differentiated colours, demonstrating that the art of tile painting in Portugal at that time equalled that of the Spanish and Italian masters.

Crucifixion, São Roque

At certain places in the church, comparatively simple and predominantly blue and white tiles can be found, which by a clever play of light and shade, create a three-dimensional effect. These tiles were imported from Seville in 1596.

Interior detail, São Roque

On the left is the fourth side chapel, **São João Baptista** (St John the Baptist) and this is the best known of São Roque's eight chapels. It was built in Rome in 1742 on the instructions of João V, shipped to Lisbon in 1747 and then carefully reassembled. Only the finest materials were used, including alabaster, amethyst, jasper, lapis lazuli, gold, silver and jewels. The pictures are not painted but are mosaics created from coloured stones. The chapel demonstrates the outstanding skills of Italian craftsmen of the mid-18th century.

There are some rather over-enthusiastic guides in São Roque who wish to speed visitors round the various sights without giving time for a close examination of its treasures. A small gratuity to the guide is probably the best way to ensure an unimpeded tour, but first ask for the lights to be switched on.

Museum exhibit

Immediately next to the church is the **Museu de Arte Sacra** (Museum of Sacred Art). Included among its exhibits are the work of Italian goldsmiths, some 17th-century paintings and pieces from the chapel of São João Baptista. Opening times: Tuesday to Sunday 10am–noon and 2–5pm. Closed Monday and holidays.

Continue up Rua da Misericórdia, the road which separates Trindade from Bairro Alto. At number 37, just before Praça Luís de Camões, stands **Tavares Rico**, a luxury restaurant housed in an equally luxurious building fronted by an impressive canopied balcony. The superb interior dating from the turn of the century is as sumptuous as the food, but do not expect to find *nouvelle cuisine*, which has yet to find favour among Portuguese diners. Prices at this restaurant match the opulent décor.

Tavares Rico

A few yards beyond Tavares Rico on the right is Praça Luís de Camões. A statue of this Portuguese classical poet (*see page 78*) stands rather forlornly in the middle, surrounded by eight of his contemporaries, writers who have long since passed into oblivion.

Just beyond and below Praça Luís de Camões is a second, smaller square, also dedicated to a literary figure, Eça de Queirós (1845–1900), a writer of realistic society novels. The statue – not intended as a piece of comic sculpture – shows the writer as an old man cradling a young girl, the embodiment of the naked truth. There is also a shop on this square which has a wide selection of tiles. Take Rua das Flores back to Praça Luís de Camões. Route 4 (*see page 33*) through Bairro Alto could now be incorporated into this route, as it begins and ends here.

Eça de Queirós

On the eastern side of Rua da Misericórdia is **Largo do Chiado**, a square named after a lyricist friend of Camões, who, although well regarded at the time, is now generally seen as a rogue. On the left is the 16th-century Igreja do Loreto, a church built in Mannerist style and yet another example of Filippo Terzi's work. Originally used by the large Italian community, it is also known as Igreja dos Italianos. Opposite stands the Igreja da Encarnação, a church with little of particular interest, built at the end of the 19th century.

A Brasileira Café

This square in the **Chiado** quarter marks the beginning of the area which was affected by the 1988 fire. Booklovers will find plenty to interest them in the part of Chiado which remains, as bookshops and antiquarian booksellers abound. Nearby is the splendid café, **A Brasileira**, which was established in 1922 and is an ideal spot for some refreshment, but it has to be *uma bica* (an expresso). Almost all Portuguese people who travel abroad are astonished to discover just how expensive a cup of coffee can be, as they regard it as a staple part of their diet.

Opposite A Brasileira, Rua dos Duques de Bragança leads to the **Teatro Nacional de São Carlos**, the earliest and probably the finest classical building in Portugal. It was built between 1792 and 1795 by José de Costa e Silva and renovated in 1940. With its well-proportioned exterior matching a moderately elegant interior, it is an ideal setting for the Portuguese opera company and for other musical performances.

Teatro Nacional de São Carlos

After passing the opera house, take a few steps along Rua Serpa Pinto to admire the facade of the old Franciscan monastery (now the Lisbon Art Academy and a library), which stretches from the opera house as far as Largo da Academia Nacional de Belas Artes. Take Rua Capelo and Rua Ivens through to this quiet square, which is surrounded on all sides by 18th- and 19th-century buildings. The Tágide is an expensive, but elegantly furnished, restaurant, with a ★ fine view over Baixa and the castle, but the same view can be seen free from the entrance to houses 12–13.

The route now follows an undulating path along Rua Vítor Cordon. The Casa do Minho has a similar function to Casa do Alentejo (*see page 18*) but is not very inviting and the dignified restaurant-bar on the ground floor has a 'Sleeping Beauty' quality about it. Next, turn right into Rua António M. Cardoso. The building with the lion-head door handles was Salazar's secret police headquarters. They were originally known as the PIDE, later the DGS. After the revolution of 25 April some of the officers who had sought shelter there fired on the crowd which had gathered outside. Four people were killed and they are commemorated by a memorial plaque.

Lion-head door handle

Further along this street is the Teatro São Luíz, which was opened in 1894 as a municipal theatre. It later burnt down but was faithfully rebuilt in 1916 and it still radiates an old-fashioned charm. Praça do Chiado stands at the top of the gently sloping Rua Garrett, the quarter's main shopping street, but it was this district which was worst affected by the fire and many smart but old-fashioned shops with fine interiors were damaged.

Magazine kiosk, Chiado

Shortly before the fire, Chiado was beginning to suffer from the competition of a new shopping centre, which had recently opened a little further away from the city centre. The reconstruction of the quarter is now going ahead under the internationally acclaimed architect Siza Vieira and it is unthinkable that he will simply copy the style of the damaged buildings. It is to be hoped that an architect with his reputation will resist the pressure of land speculators for high-rise office blocks. It is important that Chiado retains its original character.

A temporary passageway enables pedestrians to get to the city centre across the fire-damaged area. The eastern end of this bridge leads to the Carmo lift and the finishing point of this route.

Construction in Chiado

Route 4

★ Bairro Alto – Bica (*see map on page 14*)

House in Bairro Alto

This route begins and ends in Praça Luís de Camões (*see page 31*), but there is an alternative finishing point at Cais de Sodré station. The walk is not too demanding. It should be remembered that performances at *fado* house do not usually start before 10pm and many start as late as midnight.

In ★ **Bairro Alto**, the upper town, the effects of the earthquake were nowhere near as devastating as in Baixa and there are still many older buildings to be seen. The district has few sights of interest to tourists and it is the sense of a close-knit community that is most likely to be remembered. Like Alfama, the residents of Bairro Alto belong to the lower income groups and many of the buildings which from a distance look so picturesque are, in fact, badly in need of repair and renovation; much of the infrastructure is also in poor condition. Craftsmen can be seen at work in their workshops, with perhaps a couple of apprentices. Dingy shops which are not more than cellars sell a few basic food items. *Tascas* and small bars offer basic food, as well as the obligatory glass of wine. But, on the other hand, the district has adapted well to the tourists and *lisboetas*, who think that the quarter is fashionable. Enterprising shopkeepers and restaurants try to give the outsiders what they want and many of the bars have come to specialise in *fado* music.

Sign of fado music

Take Rua do Norte from Praça Luís de Camões, but pause for a moment on the corner and admire a fine street lamp bearing Lisbon's coat of arms (*see page 77*). Turn left and follow the parallel Rua Diário de Notícias. This street is named after a popular daily newspaper and reflects Bairro Alto's traditional links with the press and publishing industry. However, it is predominantly a residential area as can be seen by the **balconies** with their pretty wrought-iron railings, pot plants, window boxes and of course the washing flapping in the wind. In Adega do Ribatejo, at 23 Rua Diário de Notícias, the *fado* is sung in turn by members of the staff and consequently it seems a little more natural than elsewhere. Many more small restaurants and tiny bars are situated along this street and if there is a seat available, try the Bota Alta in Travessa da Queimada.

Balconies

Cross the whole quarter by Travessa da Queimada and Travessa dos Inglesinhos, which skirts round the site of a derelict church. This part of Bairro Alto is quieter and slightly more run-down. The winding Rua João Pereira da Rosa leads down into Rua do Século. The street takes its name from the building which formerly housed the editorial office of the *O Século* newspaper, built in 1913.

The painted stucco ceiling

Those who are interested in baroque churches should make a short detour by following Rua do Século to the end then bear left into Calçada do Combro, where only a few yards away stands the **Igreja dos Paulistas,** sometimes known as the Igreja de São Paulo da Serra de Ossa. The present building dates from the second half of the 18th century and is admired for its well-proportioned facade as well as for its brightly lit ★ **interior** where the richly decorated and neatly structured walls, the painted **stucco ceiling**, the gilded altars and the baroque organ combine to create a unified whole (daily 10am–noon and 2–4pm).

The fountain

Follow Rua do Século to the north and look for the large **fountain** on the right-hand side. It is believed to be the work of the architect Carlos Mardel, but sadly it is no longer functioning. On the other side of the street stands the **Palácio dos Carvalhos** or Palácio Pombal, which predates the earthquake, and was the birthplace in 1699 of Sebastião José de Carvalho e Melo, later to become Marquês de Pombal. It was also his home in later life when he became prime minister. Not only was Pombal the energetic rebuilder of Lisbon's devastated centre and the head of a major trading nation, but he was also tough and merciless with many of his aristocratic opponents.

The palace in its present form is also the work of Carlos Mardel, who made some alterations after the earthquake. The kerbstone for the horse-drawn coach is still visible under the gateway. The small bridge, which crosses the adjoining Rua da Academia das Ciências, used to link the palace with its garden. It is easy to forget that this quiet street is only a few hundred yards away from the centre of a busy capital city.

Business premises, Rua do Século

Walk up Rua do Século to the Constitutional Court on the left-hand side, where rows of trees line the courtyard. A few yards further on stands the dignified Convento da Conceição dos Cardais with two small, decorated porches. Formerly a Carmelite monastery dating from 1681, it survived the earthquake more or less unscathed. The interior is decorated with Portuguese and Delft tiles and attributed to Dutch artist Jan van Dort. For a hundred years, part of the spacious building was used to accommodate the blind, but at present the building is in poor condition and closed to the public. Plans are in hand to renovate it and put it to good use.

Praça do Príncipe Real

At the end of Rua do Século is the **Praça do Príncipe Real,** a park rather than a square, and an ideal spot for a rest. The smart buildings which surround the *praça* date from 1860, around the same time as the park itself and a time when the city was expanding rapidly. Príncipe Real was in those days a prestigious address. The park contains some exotic flora including an old cedar tree, but much more interesting is the **Botanical Garden** in Rua da Escola Politécnica. Cross Príncipe Real and follow the tram lines for about 200m as far as the large classical building belonging to the Faculdade das Ciências. On the left is the entrance to the Botanical Garden, which sweeps round in a wide arc almost to Avenida da Liberdade.

This is the part of Lisbon for antique shops and the prices compare favourably with the same type of shops in northern Europe. The route now heads south along one of the old shopping streets that links the river and Cais do Sodré station with Praça de Camões, Largo do Rato and Amoreiras. Initially this stretch of road is called Rua Dom Pedro V but it then becomes São Pedro de Alcântara. After a few minutes' walk, a thin strip of open space offers a fine ★ panoramic view over the east of the city. Directly below is Avenida da Liberdade, which leads up to the Parque Eduardo VII. The church of Nossa Senhora da Graça is situated more or less opposite and behind it the towers of São Vicente de Fora are just visible. The clearly delineated outline of the castle with its umbrella pines and cypresses dominates the skyline. Further round is the Sé and the course of the Tejo leads off to the southeast.

A few yards further on is one of the three **funicular railways** in Lisbon, the Elevador da Glória, which links the northern end of Bairro Alto with the Avenida da Liberdade. The track has been in service for more than 100 years. Directly opposite this working museum piece stands the **Palácio Ludovice**, which is named after Johann Friedrich Ludwig, a German who turned his back on his homeland to earn his living in Portugal. He designed the castle at Mafra for João V as well as this grand mid-18th-century building, where he lived with his family. The

Antique shop on Rua Dom Pedro

The panoramic view

Riding the funicular

ground floor now houses the **Port Wine Institute** where for a small sum it is possible to sample a glass or two of port, the famous sweet wine from the Douro valley – but there are more than 200 different types to choose from.

Port Wine Institute

Find Travessa da Cara, which is a few yards back on the right and return to Bairro Alto. This part of the district has a distinctly impoverished look, but there is some greenery to be seen, even if it is only on the roofs. At the end of the alleyway, turn right into Rua da Atalaia as far as Calçada do Tijolo to get a fine view of the Basílica da Estrela. Use the map on page 14 to negotiate the narrow alleys into Rua da Rosa. At the junction with Cunhal da Bola (Cannon Ball Corner) is a corner house decorated with hemispherical cannon balls, which was originally built for a rich Jewish merchant. It is said that the cannon balls were originally gold-plated.

Print shop

Rua da Rosa cuts across the district but is not so busy as the streets which run parallel. Now and then the sound of an old-fashioned printing press may be heard, but a few small boutiques have started to appear among the traditional shops. An old mansion, now a bank, marks the end of the street, followed by the lively Largo Calhariz. Turn left back into Praça Luís de Camões, the starting point for this route.

Bica

This tour could well be extended into the quiet Bica quarter, in which case cross Largo Calhariz to the upper station of another of Lisbon's funicular railways, the Elevador da Bica. This has been in operation since 1892 and a notice inside the carriage informs passengers how they should stand in order to maintain the correct equilibrium. Although the railway is tempting, it may be more worthwhile to descend Rua da Bica de Duarte Belo on foot and look down the alleyways that lead off it. There is only the distant rumble of traffic to remind visitors that this quiet corner is part of a metropolitan city. Many of the alleys end in steps, keeping out the cars and thereby encouraging pedestrians to explore. Many of the houses along the funicular railway track date from the 17th century, with numbers 27–33 being notable examples. Turn left just before the lower station and descend the steps by **Calçada da Bica Grande** into Rua de São Paolo. Follow the tram lines as far as the São Paolo church and square, both planned and built during the Pombal years.

Calçada de Bica Grande

Turn right just beyond the church to the Mercado da Ribeira Nova, a large market hall. On the other side of the market is Cais do Sodré station, to the east of which is the busy Praça Duque de Terceira. Take Rua Bernard and Rua do Arsenal, with their busy shops, back to Baixa and the city centre.

Route 5

Avenidas Novas – ★ Gulbenkian Museum

The part of Lisbon covered by this route was built during the past two centuries and it is not as long as it appears on the map, as it starts with a journey on the Metro. On the one hand there are the opulent town houses with a style of their own. In contrast, the sober modernism of the 1930s determined the urban style of building for the Salazar years. More recently, the post-modern office blocks, now occupied mainly by banks, have completely changed the character of the district.

But that is not to say that this area has nothing to commend it. It has become a second city centre with modern hotels, shopping arcades and shops. The Gulbenkian Museum, which will be of great interest to art-lovers, is situated in this part of the city (*see page 42*).

This route starts from the Roma Metro station at the junction of Avenida de Roma and Avenida dos Estados Unidos. The surrounding area is dominated by striking, but cold and unfriendly tower blocks which date from the 1940s and 1950s. This was a time when local architects were trying to give the current architectural fashions a distinct Portuguese flavour: crude, latticed facing,

Fashionable shop windows

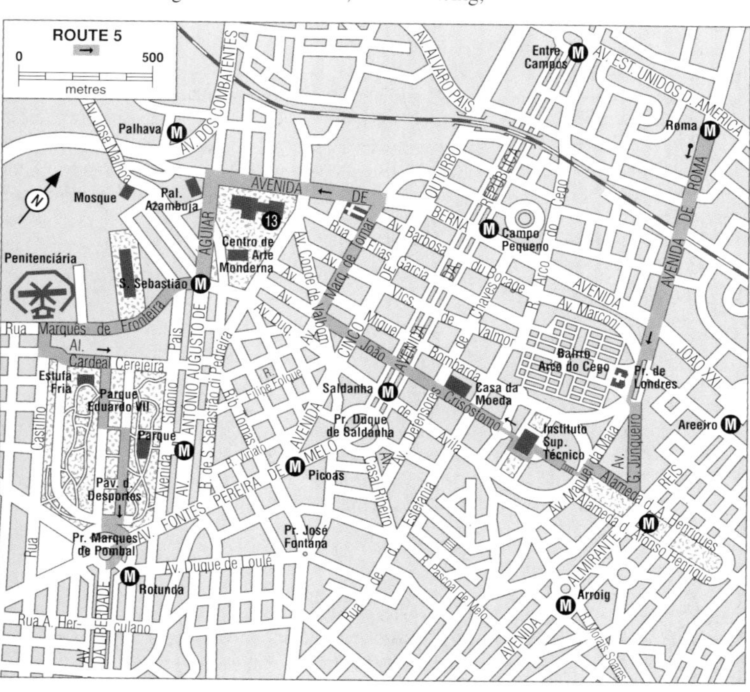

Greenery on balconies

concrete window surrounds and solid balconies characterise this district. Alvalade, the quarter to the north of this junction, was built in this style but it now has a drab appearance, as the paint peels and fades. The stark austerity of the architecture is softened only by the greenery on the balconies.

A stroll south along Avenida da Roma will reveal many elegant shops, boutiques selling fashionable shoes and clothing and home furnishing stores, which somehow seem a little out of place in this area. Now and then, however, there is an unpretentious little shop which proves that this is still a residential area and the local people still need to buy everyday items. Just beyond Ana Salazar's fashions on the left side of the road is the old Roma cinema, now looking a little shabby, and on the right are a couple of good bookshops.

New variations of the same building style are evident from an occasional glance down the side streets. The harsh effect of the concrete is lessened by some sympathetic decorative work. In Avenida da Roma itself, despite the sizeable balconies with their heavily accentuated embellishments, the houses are not unattractive. This style has its roots in the 1930s and was undoubtedly inspired by the architects of Germany's Third Reich and the Italy of Mussolini. Later on, around 1950, the Portuguese dictatorship attempted to develop its own architectural style and the showpiece can be found a little further south at **Praça de Londres**. The effect of the 11-storey office block, which dominates the square, is minimised by the tent-like roof with matching chimney stack. It is an impressive building primarily because of the pleasing dimensions and overall unity of style, but the newer adjoining glass tower block seems inappropriate. On its own it is a striking building but it is considerably taller than its neighbours and must have been designed without any regard for the effect it would have on the other edifices in the square. It serves as the Ministry of Employment.

Praça de Londres

Forty years ago, Salazar's authoritarian regime was able to plan rows of streets and squares in this style. The local authority had the power to expropriate land and property in order to extend the city. There was no restraint on these powers and they were used freely. A grand plan for the new suburbs of Lisbon was devised and implemented. The principles that guided this plan are very much in evidence on Cassiano Branco's Praça de Londres. In contrast to the impressive boulevards and avenues laid out around the turn of the century, the residential quarters were to be designed with a distinctly rural character, villages in the heart of city with detached one-family houses, a church and a school. Salazar's ideology looked back to a world where chivalry and village life were the focus for people's as-

Igreja de São João de Deus

pirations and he sought to recreate the past in these pseudo-rural settings.

Bairro do Arco Cego, the residential estate opposite Praça de Londres, was begun in the dictator's time but was extended and finished after the revolution. The bunker-like school stands at the centre of the estate contrasting with the neat semi-detached houses and tiny gardens. The **Igreja de São João de Deus** is an eye-catching structure, which was built in 1948 and stands in a prominent position at the entrance to the estate near Praça de Londres. The proportions of the tall, narrow, turreted tower contrast almost grotesquely with the unshapely body of the church. The large structure behind the church to the right is a post-modern temple of a different kind – the headquarters of a major bank completed in 1992.

Bairro do Arco Cego

There are a number of estates similar to Bairro do Arco Cego in the northern part of the city but they are to some extent more compact. Life on such an estate is clearly more appealing than in an anonymous tower block, but such housing developments, which necessitated so much land, could never hope to accommodate the huge influx of rural Portuguese who came seeking work.

To the right on Avenida Manuel de Maia is the Instituto Nacional de Estatística (National Statistics Institute). It was built in the early 1930s, designed in an appropriately functional style.

Continue the route down Avenida Guerra Junqueiro, lined on both sides by 1940s' multi-storey apartment blocks. There is little variation in the architecture. By taking a walk through the entrance to number 13a, it is possible to look behind one of these huge, identical blocks. The ugliness of the drainpipes and huge concrete staircases is offset by the soothing, albeit flaking, pastel paint which is more noticeable than on the front walls.

Concrete blocks and drainpipes

Fonte Luminosa

At the point where Avenida Guerra Junqueiro joins Alameda de Afonso Henriques, it is possible to see the pinnacle of 1940s architectural achievements. A look at the map clarifies the planners' intentions: the Instituto Superior Técnico situated to the right on a hill looks down over the extensive park from inside a horseshoe-shaped arc. At the lower end of the park, a huge fountain, the **Fonte Luminosa**, completes the overall effect. The **Cinema Império**, which can boast a facade to match its name, is situated opposite: it's a real film palace. The pillars at the entrance are crowned with two armillary spheres, models of the celestial sphere, consisting of intertwined rings representing the relative position of the ecliptic and the celestial equator. This instrument was used by early astronomers for determining the position of the stars and during the reign of Manuel I, the armillary sphere came to represent the years of Portuguese expansion. The Empire Cinema clearly sought to evoke the nation's imperial past. It was designed by Cassiano Branco, the architect of Praça de Londres.

Walk up the slope to the Instituto Superior Técnico. This severe building preceded the cinema and dates from the 1930s. It is usually possible to cross the campus (if closed, then a short detour is required) to reach Avenida João Crisóstomo, a quiet avenue. On the left is the tram depot, but it is only possible to take a look inside from the other direction. Opposite to the right is the mint, the Casa da Moeda, another austere piece of functional architecture built in the 1930s.

Café Versailles

Follow Avenida João Crisóstomo and cross the wide **Avenida da República**. The impact which this grand boulevard must have made in earlier years has been destroyed by the construction of modern offices and residential accommodation. Only one of the original buildings remains unchanged and that can be seen opposite. Most of the blocks were built during the first two decades of the 20th century. The flourishing style may not be to everyone's taste, but the imaginative facades have a certain charm. A good choice for a break might be the **Café Versailles** at number 15 with its tastefully decorated old-style interior. Customers have the choice of serving themselves at the bar or waiting to be served at a table.

Continue along Avenida João Crisóstomo and and take the second turning on the right into Avenida Marquês de Tomar. At the far end is the **Igreja do Rosário de Fátima**. Consecrated in 1938, it was the first church to be built in a modern style. Some well-known Portuguese architects and artists contributed to the controversial design. Of special interest are Almada Negreiros' stained-glass windows and also his mosaic in the baptistry. Opening times: 8.30am–noon and 4.30–7pm.

Behind the Igreja do Rosário de Fátima runs Avenida de Berna; diagonally opposite and set back a little from the road is the Curry Cabral, a home for 'fallen' women built in the 18th century. On the left is the entrance to the **Parque Gulbenkian ⓭**. This park consists of the well-known museum, a library, administrative buildings and the Centro de Arte Moderna (*see page 43*). Praça de Espanha and the busy junction in the northwest corner of the park are presently undergoing major alterations.

On the western side of Avenida António Augusto de Aguiar stands the handsome Palácio Azambuja dating from 1660. This building now houses the Spanish embassy and consequently it is well guarded and not open to visitors. The square structure with a dome and tower behind the palace is the new mosque (1980).

Follow Avenida António Augusto de Aguiar back towards the city centre and on the right look for Bairro Azul, the blue quarter. It is of interest from an architectural point of view, as it was here in the 1930s that the distinct lines of modern architecture were linked with the decorative elements of art deco. On the right, Rua Marquês de Fronteira leads uphill, where two imposing villas can be seen: **Palacete Leitão** at numbers 14–16 (it may be necessary to find a higher position in order to get a good view); and the Palacete Mendonça at numbers 18–28. Both buildings were constructed at the beginning of the 20th century. From here the rear of Parque Eduardo VII is visible. The Câmara Municipal (City Council) is now planning a further extension to the parkland on the open land to the left, although at one time it seemed that this area had already been earmarked by land speculators.

On the right stand the bleak Ministry of Justice and a **prison**, the Penitenciária with a ground plan that has for a long time been the standard model for such institutions. The outer perimeter is hexagonal and a central observation and supplies post overlooks the six wings, which then form smaller exercise yards. With this design, it takes only a short time for central control to reach any cell in the building and furthermore it is easy to isolate a section of the 100-year-old prison should any trouble occur.

The **Parque Eduardo VII** also dates from the end of the last century. It is named after the English king, Edward VII, who made a state visit to Lisbon in 1903. The 40 hectares (100 acres) of open space at the northern end of Avenida da Liberdade compensate for the claustrophobic city streets. At the upper end of the park is a viewing terrace with lamps and concrete pillars which date from around 1940. The ★ **view** from the terrace can, on a clear day, extend as far as the Palmela mountains.

There are two places of interest on the eastern side of the park. First there is the ★ **Estufa Fria**, a 'cold green-

Sculpture in the park

Palacete Leitão

Prison sign

Parque Eduardo VII

A pond in the Estufa Fria

house', with tropical plants and a large number of cacti. It is described as 'cold', as there is no roof. Adjacent is the **Estufa Quente** (hothouse), whose plants need higher temperatures. In the summer, the Estufa Fria is sometimes illuminated. Opening times: 9am–5.30pm.

To the south of the greenhouse is the Pavilhão dos Desportos – its official name is Pavilhão Carlos Lopes after an Olympic marathon runner. Although it was built only in 1932, it imitates an earlier style and is decorated with some fine *azulejos*. It is now used as a venue for concerts and large meetings.

Statue of Marquês de Pombal

The statue on a tall plinth at the southern end of the park depicts the Marquês de Pombal. Two foundation stones were laid: one in 1917, a second in 1926 and the statue was not finally finished until 1934. It now stands rather forlornly in the middle of one of the city's busiest junctions, Praça Marquês de Pombal, or the Rotunda as it is usually known. At the base of the statue is a large replica of the city's coat of arms, made from coloured stones. A number of these coats of arms can be found at various points around the city. For many years they were neglected, but there has recently been some talk of restoring them.

To return to the city centre, either catch the Metro from the Rotunda station or take a leisurely stroll down Avenida da Liberdade.

Museu Calouste Gulbenkian

⋆ Museu Calouste Gulbenkian

To visit the museum quarter, but not as part of *Route* 5, take the Metro to São Sebastião station, then walk up Avenida Augusto de Águiar to the Gulbenkian Foundation park. From October to May the museum is open from Tuesday to Sunday 10am–5pm; from June to September, Sunday, Tuesday, Thursday, Friday 10am–5pm, Wednesday and Saturday 2–7pm.

The life story of Calouste Gulbenkian sounds more like fiction than fact. Born an Armenian in Constantinople in 1869, he became an immensely rich oil magnate and used his fortune to build up a prestigious art collection. During World War II, his fortune was threatened because he had become an Iranian citizen and was therefore regarded as an opponent of the Allies. In 1942 Gulbenkian moved to Portugal, a neutral country, to safeguard his assets. After the war he continued to direct his oil empire from Lisbon. When he died in 1955 he left a large part of his wealth not to his family but to a foundation which took control of his art collection.

Gulbenkian in the park

At the time, the effects of such an eminent foundation on the cultural life of a small, relatively poor country like Portugal were inestimable. The Fundação Gulbenkian funds a top-class orchestra, a choir and a ballet company. It also encourages young artists by awarding generous grants and by buying works of art. The Foundation also makes contributions to social projects. Presidents of the Foundation are always highly respected and influential citizens of Lisbon.

The Museu Calouste Gulbenkian was opened in 1969 and behind its rather severe facade are untold treasures. The park in which it is set has its own charm and is an ideal spot for a restful stroll. Not all of Gulbenkian's acquisitions are exhibited here. Some may be seen in the Museu de Arte Antiga (*see page 52*).

Gulbenkian had a broad interest in the arts and the exhibits are wide-ranging, from Ancient Egyptian to Greek and Roman art, supplemented by a collection of ancient coins. As well as medieval book illustrations, works from the Middle and Far East, the museum has a fine collection of carpets, furniture, porcelain and silver. A whole section is devoted to art nouveau pieces by Lalique. Some of the exhibits here were commissioned by Gulbenkian himself as he enjoyed a long friendship with the French artist, René Lalique (1860–1945). Other important names from the world of European art are also represented here. The collection of works by the Venetian artists Antonio and Francesco Guardi is well known, and a few works by Manet and Degas are on display here too.

Manet's Boy Blowing Bubbles

Special exhibitions are held in an adjoining wing and there is a cafeteria and a library in the basement. In the library reading room is a passable likeness of Gulbenkian himself as an old man.

The **Centro de Arte Moderna** was opened on the same site in 1984 and it has more to offer in an architectural sense than the main building. It houses 20th-century Portuguese paintings including the works of the Expressionist Amadeu Sousa Cardoso and a portrait of the poet Pessoa by Almada Negreiros.

Historic buildings in Belém

Route 6

★★★ Belém – ★★★ Jerónimos Monastery

Belém is a shortened form of Bethlehem. Lying on the bank of the Tejo, this western suburb of Lisbon was incorporated into the city in 1885. Belém developed from the earlier harbour of Restelo, from where the caravels set sail on their voyages of discovery. In the later Middle Ages, the busy coastal town became the centre of Portugal's expanding world empire. Many of the important buildings which now symbolise the town's historic past were constructed during the reign of Manuel I (1495–1521) and were unaffected by the 1755 earthquake. Visitors to Belém should beware of pickpockets and camera thieves. There has also been an alarming rise in the number of thefts by young moped riders.

The No. 15 tram

Belém is well served by public transport. The easiest way to get to there is by the 15 or 17 tram from the eastern end of Praça do Comércio. The 16 tram and 28 bus pass Santa Apolónia station, and tram 17 and bus 43 pass Praça Figueira. The 27 and 49 buses leave for Belém from Praça Marquês de Pombal. There is also a suburban train every 20 minutes from Cais do Sodré station, but check on the departure board whether the train stops in Belém.

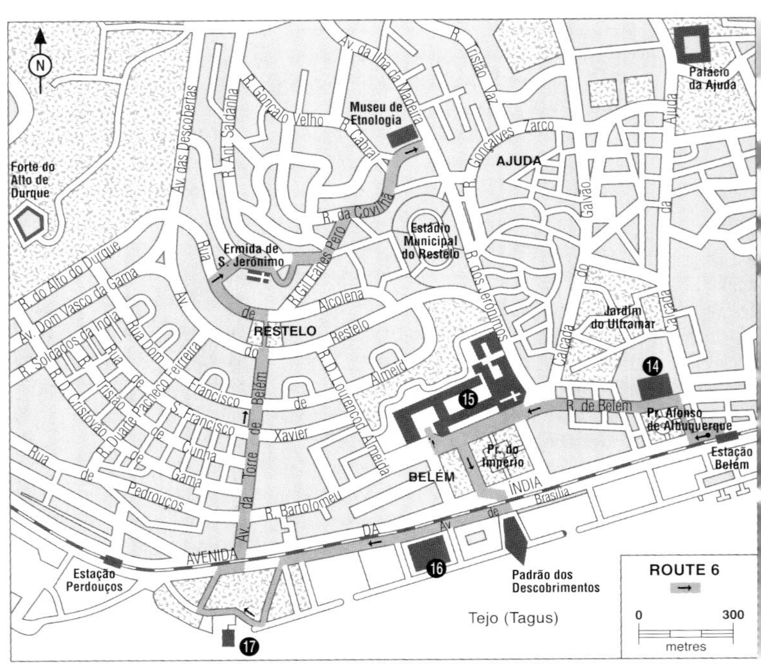

Only yards away, to the east of Belém station, is a large brick-built construction with four large chimneys. It is the Central Tejo, a coal-powered electricity station which was converted into an industrial museum in 1990. In addition to the collections of old electric motors and devices and a display documenting the history of Lisbon's power supply, all the old power station's technical equipment may be viewed. Opening times: Tuesday to Sunday 10am–12.30pm and 2–6pm. Closed Monday and holidays.

On the western side of the railway station is Praça Afonso de Albuquerque, a small park named after the first Portuguese viceroy of India. In the centre of the park stands a neo-Manueline pillar bearing a bronze statue of the Portuguese hero (1902).

The Presidential Palace

On the north side of the park are two grand buildings: in the background is the pink-washed Palácio de Belém, sometimes known as the Palácio Cor de Rosa, and this is the official residence of the Portuguese president. It was founded in the 16th century by Manuel I, but has undergone many alterations, mostly since it was purchased by João V in 1726. The royal family were here when the earthquake struck and they were unharmed.

In front of the presidential palace is the old royal riding school which now houses the ★ **Museu Nacional dos Coches** (National Coach Museum) ⓮. The old coaches are displayed in rather unimaginative straight lines and there is little in the way of background information on the exhibits. However, the range of gilded and painted carriages with their satin interiors is impressive. Most coaches date from the 18th century and display characteristic baroque embellishments. One of the older coaches at the start of the left-hand row is simply decorated. It was constructed at the end of the 16th century for Filipe II, one of Portugal's Spanish rulers (*see page 10*). It was only later that the monarchy's love of splendour was applied to the design of royal carriages. The pinnacle of the art was achieved with the three Italian coaches built for the Grand Legation led by the Marquis of Fontes to Pope Clement XI. Look for the imposing groups of carved and gilded writhing figures in the Italian baroque style. Also on show are smaller processional coaches for carrying pictures of saints, and sedan chairs which are carried by men or mules. Opening times: Tuesday to Sunday 10am–1pm and 2.30–5.30pm. Closed Monday and holidays.

Symbolic figure on a coach

Follow Rua de Belém, in front of the museum, and admire the view of one of Portugal's most impressive buildings, the **Jerónimos Monastery**. But beforehand, make a detour to the left into Travessa da Praça and walk along the delightful Rua Vieira Portuense, which runs parallel to Rua de Belém. The whole street with its narrow, modest houses dates from the 16th and 17th century.

View of the Jerónimos Monastery

The west porch

The cupola

★★★ **Jerónimos Monastery** ⓯ (Mosteiro dos Jerón imos). Opening times: Tuesday to Sunday 10am–1pm an 2.30–5pm. The monastery dates from the first half of th 16th century and at that time was situated next to the Tej but with the building of the harbour basin and the alte ation in the course of the river, the river bank has move to the south. The choice of site can be traced back to Henr the Navigator who built a small chapel, the Nossa Senhor de Restelo, at the time of the first great voyages of dis covery. Only 20 years ago the cod fishermen used to re ceive a blessing here before setting out on their long fishin expeditions in the spring. The monastery was built o the initiative of Manuel I, who ruled an empire many time the size of Portugal. It is thought that the work began i 1502 after Vasco da Gama's successful voyage to India

There have been very few changes; the tower had pointed roof before it was replaced with a **cupola** an the western section of the long monastery building, whic now houses an archaeological and maritime museum, wa rebuilt and restored in neo-Manueline style.

The first architect and designer of the complex was Boy tac, whose nationality is unknown, but he was eithe French, Italian or Portuguese. After 1517, the Spaniar Castilho continued working on the project but with the as sistance of the Frenchman Chanterène and later Dieg de Torralva and Jean de Rouen. Although it was not finall completed until 1572, there is an extraordinary architec tural unity in evidence throughout the complex. The ubiq uitous Manueline ornaments mask the fact that th construction of the complex straddled the late Gothic an Renaissance periods.

The ★★ southern portal of the Igreja de Santa Mari church, undergoing restoration at the time of going t press, is one of the finest examples of Manueline archi tecture. Not only is it wide enough to incorporate two adjacent buttresses, but it also reaches up as far as the filigree-style balustrade on the edge of the roof. Between the two doors in a canopied niche stands a statue of Henry the Navigator, which is not thought to be a life-like portrayal. Above the door arch is a madonna and right at the top an angel bearing a coat of arms. The reliefs above the two doorways portray scenes from the life of St Jerónimus. There is not one section of the whole portal which is not a perfect illustration of the elaborate, twisting and spiralling Manueline style.

Another example can be seen on the relatively simple windows: there is no line which is not twisted, no surface which is left plain and empty. Take a close look and try to follow the intricate filigree patterns, which are often, and not by accident, in arabesque style.

Detail of the west porch

The ★★ west porch by Nicolas Chanterène is much less impressive, partly because it stands in the shade of the monastery. Scenes from Bethlehem (Belém) can be seen on the tympanum: the birth of Christ and the adoration of the shepherds. Depicted to the left, next to the door, are Manuel I and his patron saint St Jerónimus and on the right, his wife Maria of Castille and her patron saint St John the Baptist. The faces of the royal couple are said to be close likenesses.

Vaulted roof of the transept

Inside the church, the nave and side aisles all of a uniform height, and the graceful octagonal pillars supporting the Gothic fan vault combine to create a stunning effect, while the dimensions of the ★★ transept speak for themselves: 25m (80ft) high by 19m (60ft) wide and 29m (90ft) long. The weight of the roof is supported by the ribbed vaulting fanning out above the pillars at the intersection and happily this bold construction survived the earthquake. The eye is deceived by the pillars which appear narrower because of the Manueline decorations – vines, shoots and strange creatures. Rays of sunlight streaming through the stained-glass windows can create a beautiful effect. It is only the Renaissance choir which spoils the overall unity of the interior.

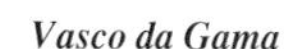
Vasco da Gama

On the left by the entrance is a tombstone honouring **Vasco da Gama** (*see page* 5) and on the right another commemorates Luis de Camões (*see page78*). Both were built during the 19th century in neo-Manueline style. It is not known where Camões' remains actually lie, but it is suspected that at the time of his death the impoverished and virtually forgotten poet was buried in a mass grave for plague victims. In the choir on the left beneath a tombstone supported by elephants lie King Manuel I and his wife Maria and on the right are the graves of his successor João III and his wife Catarina. In the transept lie other tombs including those of some of the unfortunate rulers of

Manueline cloister

the House of Avis. There is an (empty) tomb for the young King Sebastião who went missing in Africa and also the grave of Cardinal Henrique, the last of the line, who came to the throne as an old man and only lasted for two years before being ousted by the Spanish in 1580.

Near the western entrance to the church is the entrance to the ★★★ **cloister**, which, together with the monastery at Batalha (*see page 70*) and the Convent of Christ in Tomar (*see page 71*), are the pinnacle of Manueline design. The lower storey is the work of Boytac and the upper of Castilho. Some people might think the cloister is an example of Manueline excess with its rich motifs from the sea and from abroad – parrots and other birds, plants and pearls set in spirals. Although not to everyone's taste, cast in stone and unadulterated are the artists' impressions of a new world as perceived by Portuguese explorers of the 15th and 16th centuries.

Detail of the cloister

The cloister leads into the chapter house, where a further four tombstones may be seen. There are two 19th-century poets Alexandre Herculano and Almeida Garrett as well as the first president of the first republic, Teófilo Braga, and Oscar Carmona, the leader of the 1926 military putsch, which later led to Salazar seizing power. Carmona became the ceremonial president of Salazar's regime, until his death in 1951.

In the western part of the monastery is the ★ **Museum Nacional de Arqueologia e Etnologia**. It houses a wide collection of valuable archaeological finds, many of which are pre-Roman, including artefacts from prehistoric and early times and a splendid collection of Celtic gold jewellery, which unfortunately is not always on display. Opening times: 10am–noon and 2–5pm.

To the right at the end of the monastery complex is the **Museu da Marinha** (Maritime Museum), which documents the history of Portuguese seafaring with a series of model ships, paintings, charts, navigational aids, etc. Also included in the collection are models of the boats used on Portugal's rivers and deep-sea fishing vessels. Two old seaplanes are also exhibited here, one of which, the Santa Cruz, was used by Gago Coutinho and Sacadura Cabral for a crossing of the Atlantic from Lisbon to Rio de Janeiro in 1922. Opening times: Tuesday to Sunday 10am–5pm. Closed Monday and holidays.

Maritime Museum exhibit

Turn back towards the river and look over the site which was prepared for the 1940 'Exhibition of the Portuguese World'. Conceived at great expense by the government, this exercise in propaganda was designed by the architect Cottineli Telmo. The year 1940 was important for Portugal, as it represented the 300th anniversary of the country's independence from Spain. Praça do Império (Imperial Square) was also laid out at that time and it displays in stone and trimmed hedges the coats of arms of Portugal's cities. On the right is the controversial Centro Cultural de Belém which was completed in 1991. It is due to house a museum documenting the voyages of discovery.

Padrão dos Descobrimentos

A subway leads to the ★ **Padrão dos Descobrimentos**, (Discoveries Monument), an angular monument to the discoveries, which was originally constructed for the 1940 exhibition and then dismantled. In 1960, it was re-erected in its present form with a compass, which was a gift from the Republic of South Africa, built into the stone in front of the monument. Since 1985, several rooms inside the monument have been furnished and these are now used for small temporary exhibitions or conferences on the subject of the discoveries.

The Padrão dos Descobrimentos is built in the shape of the bows of a caravel. Led by Henry the Navigator, stylised figures look defiantly out over the Tejo. Created by the sculptor Leopoldo de Almeida, these over-sized figures resemble other heroic statues popular with dictators and authoritarian regimes. There is some irony attached to the date, as it was only one year after the monument was unveiled that the collapse of the Portuguese empire began. India occupied and then annexed the colony of Goa and the guerilla wars of liberation started in Africa.

Fishing in the River Tejo

A lift gives access to a viewing platform at the top of the monument with a marvellous view over the Tejo bridge and the Belém itself. The huge building to the right behind the monastery is the Palácio da Ajuda (*see page 53*).

To the west of the monument is a restaurant called Espelho de Agua (Water Mirror), which is housed in a building surrounded by water. It too was constructed as part of the world exhibition and was designed by Cottineli

Museum of Popular Art

Telmo. Another of Telmo's work is the **Museu de Arte Popular ⑯**, the museum of popular art, which contains a collection of Portuguese crafts grouped according to the various provinces. Unfortunately, the exhibits are not well labelled and no background information is provided. The rooms which contain murals created around 1940 by well-known contemporary artists are currently closed due to renovation work.

Walk in a westerly direction past the harbour basin. The run-down factory buildings on the right side of the busy highway make a depressing sight. One of Portugal's best known landmarks, the ★★ **Tower of Belém ⑰** will perhaps remind visitors that the country has known wealth and power. It is situated behind a small park at the point where the River Tejo widens into a bay. The tower was conceived as a lighthouse and defensive fortress and originally stood on an island, where it must have cut a more elegant figure. It was commissioned by Manuel I in 1515 but by the beginning of the 19th century it had been partly destroyed. Fortunately it was restored to its original condition in 1845.

The Tower of Belém

Francisco de Arruda was the man responsible for its construction. Before setting to work on the project, he spent many years working in Portuguese territory on the Moroccan coast and had been influenced greatly by Moorish art. He had also learnt a great deal from his older brother Diogo de Arruda, who was also an architect and an enthusiastic exponent of Manueline art. These different influences explain the tower's unusual mixture of Manueline and Arab styles.

Battlements, Tower of Belém

The structure consists of a tower and a bastion facing towards the river, with embrasures incorporated into the battlement walls. Between the embrasures and the battlements, formed by the juxtaposition of coats of arms, run two stone ropes which are knotted in front of the towers. Ropes and knots were, of course, typical elements of Manueline decorations. The coats of arms bear the cross of the Knights of Christ.

The six small domed watch-towers are reminiscent of Islamic architecture, as are the two oriel windows on the side of the tower which faces land and the four small domed towers crowning the four corners. Below one small tower on the right-hand side, a rhinoceros' horn is just visible. According to legend, in 1513 King Manuel I received a rhinoceros as a present from India. The unusual animal, unknown in Europe at that time, aroused considerable interest. But many people wondered which animal was stronger, a rhinoceros or an elephant, and so they were placed face to face on Praça do Império to find out. The elephant fled in fear and, as a result, Manuel decided to give Pope Leo X a rhinoceros as a present. However, on its way to Rome, the ship carrying the animal sank in the Tyrrhenian Sea.

A coat of arms

From land the tower looks well fortified with its double-arched windows and neat roofed balconies, but the side which looks out over the river with the seven-arched loggia and other decorative elements has a more elegant look to it. A Portuguese **coat of arms** can be seen above the loggia with the ornate stone balustrade. At the same level, one on each side, are two armillary spheres, symbols of the country's maritime achievements. A close look at the wall will reveal several layers of twisted ropes surrounding the tower, separating the various floors. On the bastion terrace stands a Gothic madonna, Nossa Senhora de Belém or Nossa Senhora de Bom Sucesso (Our Lady of Safe Voyages).

Street signpost

The inside of the tower is sober and functional with few adornments. The ground floor and cellar were used for provisions and arms. A spiral staircase leads to the Governor's Chamber and then the King's Chamber, the *Sala Régia*. The floor above served as the audience chamber and above that there was a small chapel. Opening times: winter Tuesday to Sunday 10am–1pm and 2.30–5pm; summer 10am–6.30pm.

Those who need to return to the city centre quickly can catch a train from the nearby Pedrouços station. For those with sufficient time and energy, a stroll up Avenida da Torre de Belém to the small Ermida de São Jerónimo (Chapel of St Jeronimus; *see page 52*) and then on to the Museu de Etnologia (Museum of Ethnology; *see page 52*) is recommended. The walk takes about 30 minutes.

Ermida de São Jerónimo

Additional Sights and Museums

This section covers those sights not included in the six routes. It starts from Belém and then moves east. A good street plan will usually give the exact locations.

Firstly, some information on two minor places of interest near Belém:

Capela da Santo Amaro. This small chapel, situated near the busy access roads to the Tejo bridge, is often closed. Santo Amaro was built in 1549 in Renaissance style. It is a round chapel with a cupola and semi-circular porch, decorated with some interesting *azulejos* showing patterns of interwoven flowers, birds and angels.

Ermida de São Jerónimo, Belém (*see map on page 44*). Probably designed by Boytac in 1514, this small chapel was built on an extensive site near the Jerónimos Monastery but unfortunately it is often closed. It can be reached on foot from the other sights in Belém. A monolithic structure, it stands out from nearby buildings because of its balanced dimensions, a common feature of Manueline design. The ornamentation is restrained when set beside the monastery or the Tower of Belém; the corner pillars jut out beyond the building tapering to a fine point and the portal is attractive with its slender cross. All these elements combine to add elegance to the simple, but well-proportioned building.

Exhibit, Museu de Etnologia

The church and the hill beyond provide an unusual view of the Tower of Belém below. The ★ **Museu de Etnologia**, Belém (*see map on page 44*) is a 10-minute walk from here. The Museum of Ethnology houses some 25,000 items, many of which were brought back from former colonies by Portuguese travellers. Despite the opening of an annex in 1985, there is still insufficient space for any permanent exhibitions. The quality of the displays can be variable; some of the most interesting exhibits are presented with only minimal explanation, others are shown in context and fully documented. Opening times: Tuesday to Sunday 10.30am–6pm. Closed Monday and holidays. 15 minutes' walk from Belém's Praça do Império or number 15 bus from the Rossio.

Palácio da Ajuda

Palácio da Ajuda, Largo da Ajuda, Belém (*see map on page 44*). The Portuguese royal family residences have been dogged by bad luck. The first one was destroyed in the 1755 earthquake and its successor in the district of Ajuda was burnt down in 1795. The third one, the Palácio da Ajuda, which was started in 1802, was never completely finished, as the Portuguese royal family was forced to flee to Brazil in 1807 as Napoleonic troops approached. It was not until the end of the 19th century that it became habitable, and then with only half of the original plan completed. In contrast to the impressive facade, gaping holes at the rear serve as windows. Some Portuguese critics have seen the building as in some way symbolising the decline of the nation. An architectural competition is underway and with the help of some finance from a foundation, whose funds accrue from the profits of a Macao gambling casino, an end is in sight to the long and unfortunate saga surrounding this site.

Classical interior of the palace

The huge construction, built in classical style, appears compact and strong. A part of the spacious accommodation houses the Ministry for the Protection of Ancient Monuments and also the Secretariat for Administrative Reform. Some rooms are used for state receptions and can usually be visited. In the hallway stand statues by 19th-century sculptors including Machado de Castro. It is fascinating to see how lavishly the royal family lived, and to pass through their quarters, still complete with carpets, furniture and paintings. Opening times: Monday to Sunday 10am–5pm. Closed Wednesday and holidays. Tram number 18 from Praça do Comércio or number 14 bus from Praça da Figueira.

Diagonally opposite the rear of the palace is the entrance to the small but very attractive Ajuda Botanical Garden, which was laid out in the 18th century.

★★ **Museu Nacional de Arte Antiga.** The National Museum of Ancient Art is situated in Rua das Janelas Verdes and is sometimes referred to as *Casa das Janelas Verdes*, or the House of Green Windows. The oldest part of the building was originally a villa built by Count Alvor in 1690, but it later became the property of one Sebastião José de Carvalho or the Marquês de Pombal as he later became known, who had the windows painted green, hence the name of the villa and the street. The windows are no longer green and the building has been subject to many changes and alterations over the centuries.

Museu Nacional de Arte Antiga

The museum has been undergoing more changes and so it is impossible to describe precisely the location of some of the exhibits. Certainly worth visiting is the collection of gold and silver dating from between the 12th and 19th century. Among the prized possessions are the processional cross commissioned by King Sancho I in 1214 and the ★ **Custódia de Belém**, the famous Monstrance of Belém, which Gil Vicente is said to have created for Manuel I in 1506. The gold used in this monstrance was brought back from India by Vasco da Gama on his second voyage.

The vast collection of sculptures includes the portrayals of the pregnant Mary (Senhora da Ó), but the highlight of this museum is without doubt the collection of Portuguese paintings dating from the 15th and 16th centuries. Apart from a number of anonymous masters, many great works of Nuño Gonçalves, Jorge Afonso, Frey Carlos, Gregório Lopes, Cristovão de Figueira and Gaspar Vaz are exhibited here.

Details from the polyptych of St Vincent

The ★★ **polyptych of St Vincent** attributed to Nuño Gonçalves is a work of great artistic and historical importance. The panels were discovered in the 19th century in São Vicente de Fora (*see page 23*) and argument has raged ever since as to who painted them and when. Nuño Gonçalves, who was court painter to King Afonso V from 1450 to 1467, is thought by most people to be responsible for the six altar panels and it is assumed that they were painted around 1460. The artistic importance of the work lies in the way the characters are portrayed; they stand alone – not, as was more common, against a background of countryside or buildings. It also represents a move away from stylised portraits and points towards the emergence of a clear medieval notion of status.

In style, the polyptych demonstrates great originality and there are many factors which point to the influence of the Flemish and Italian schools. The theme of the work is the adoration of St Vincent, but it is much more than tha, as it portrays all ranks of Portuguese society. Without the

Polyptych of St Vincent

distractions of a background, concentration is focused on the faces of the characters, which show a wide range of expressions.

This polyptych has become hugely popular, portraying so many characters from all walks of life, including several members of the royal family, many of whom can be positively identified. The panel on the far left shows some Cistercian monks, fishermen and navigators. The main panel on the left (*see illustration on page 54*) shows priests and knights gathered round St Vincent with members of the royal family in the foreground. On the right is Afonso V who reigned from 1438 to 1481 and was unable to resist the demands of the powerful nobility. His wife, Isabel is deep in thought. Standing behind the king is his son, portrayed as a small boy, who later became King João II, and, unlike his father, was able to assert his authority over the aristocracy. To the left of the boy, looking solemnly but calmly ahead, stands Prince Henry the Navigator who lived from 1394 to 1460, and was an uncle of King Afonso V. Henry was known as the Father of the Discoveries, and founded a school of navigation at Sagres, although he did very little sailing himself. This portrayal of the prince has been used as a model for countless poor-quality copies. Behind the queen is Isabel, one of Henry the Navigator's sisters and wife of the Duke of Burgundy. She was the mother of Charles the Bold, who tried in vain to create an independent Burgundian kingdom. The other personalities on this panel are knights.

The main right-hand panel shows knights and a number of spiritual leaders, including Archbishop Jaime of Lisbon, who can be identified by the mitre. On the left in front of St Vincent stands Prince Fernando, brother of Afonso and father of the future king, Manuel I. On the far right in the corner, the face of the historian Gomes Eanes de Zurara is clearly visible. Many experts believe that the tall, bald-headed figure beside him is a self-portrait of the artist.

The other panels on the right show various representatives of the aristocracy. On the extreme right, a cleric is holding the remains of St Vincent, and behind him stands a Jewish scholar with the Torah. The names attributed to the characters are based on reliable historical sources, but in many cases it is impossible to be absolutely certain of their identity.

The main sections of the museum are devoted to works of European but non-Portuguese origin: furniture, porcelain, gold and silver (mainly from the 18th century), and also some sculptures from the Calouste Gulbenkian Foundation including a handsome Greco-Egyptian lion dating from Ptolemaic times, a statue of Apollo and a piece by Auguste Rodin.

Isabel is deep in thought

Henry the Navigator

The collection of European paintings should not be missed. It contains works by Zurbarán, Ribera, Memling, Dürer *(St Jeronimus)* and Holbein the Elder. But Hieronymus Bosch's masterpiece, the ★★ *Altar and Temptation of St Anthony* is one of the museum's most important works. The central panel contains some of Bosch's wildest and darkest images. It is swarming with demons and strange beings, allusions and innuendoes whose significance is difficult to unravel. Even art historians cannot agree about the picture's meaning. It is possible to go behind the altar and study the desolate black and white Golgotha scenes. These panels were originally only shown when the altar was closed during Lent.

Temptation of St Anthony

Changing exhibitions are held in the basement, which also leads to the small but excellent cafeteria. There is a garden with a fine view over the Tejo and both the garden and the cafeteria are open at lunch-time.

Opening times: Tuesday to Sunday 10am–1pm and 2.30–5pm. Closed Monday and holidays. Take the number 40 bus from Praça da Figueira, or catch bus number 25, get off in Rua São João da Mata and walk the last part of the journey up Rua das Janelas Verdes. (The 25 bus links up with the Basílica da Estrela; *see below*.) The district which lies between here and the city is the old mariners' quarter of Madragoa, meaning the Mother of Goa, the former Portuguese colony on the west coast of India. For those with time to spare, this lively part of Lisbon contains some good-value restaurants and is well worth exploring in more detail.

Basílica da Estrela

At the lower end of Rua São João da Mata, turn right into Rua das Janelas Verdes. On the right-hand side, set back a little from the road, is the Convento dos Marianos, designed by Terzi in 1606. Just before the museum, take a quick look at number 70–78, a house decorated with some fine *azulejos* from the turn of the century.

Facade detail, Basílica da Estrela

Basílica da Estrela, Largo da Estrela, Lapa. The construction of this church, which is dedicated to the Sacred Heart of Jesus, is closely linked with the fate of Queen Dona Maria I. She was the first-born daughter of King Dom José, who was overshadowed by his prime minister, Pombal. Maria had no brothers and was therefore the heir to the throne. When she married in 1760, she vowed to build a church if she bore a son and thus a successor. Son José was born, but work did not start immediately on the promised church. Only when Maria ascended the throne, was the matter taken seriously. The pious queen cast the Marquês de Pombal aside and in the years which followed reasserted the power of the monarchy and the church. Two years before the Basílica was finally completed, the young prince died of smallpox. The queen showed signs of increasing instability and in 1792 her second son João, the future João VI, became regent. Maria died in 1816 in Brazil and her body was brought back to Portugal and buried in the Basílica da Estrela.

The church occupies an exposed site in the western part of the city and is regarded as the most important piece of ecclesiastical architecture from the 18th century. The late-baroque building, which incorporates some classical elements, is principally the work of Reinaldo Manuel, the successor to the original designer, Mateus Vicente, who died in 1786. The unified style of the building can be attributed to the fact that all the architects associated with its construction came from the ★ Mafra School. The Basílica da Estrela is in fact modelled on the much grander basilica at Mafra (*see page 67*).

Statue outside the Basílica

The exterior is well balanced: cupola, towers and classical portals are in harmony. The portals are fronted by elegant pillars, whose white stone radiates brightness in sunlight. The statues on the facade, as well as those inside, are the work of the Mafra School of Sculpture led by Machado de Castro. Some of the works are his, including the Mary and Joseph in the niches in the atrium.

The single-aisled nave, offset by six side chapels, has a lightness which can be attributed in part to the use of pink, white and grey marble. The altarpieces are almost all the work of the Italian Botoni. On the right in the transept lies the tomb of Maria I, but the tombstone of her father confessor, another of Machado de Castro's works, is even more richly decorated and can be found in the sacristy. Although not always open, a small chamber off the transept houses a crib by the same sculptor. Opening times: daily 9am–1pm and 3.30–8pm. Trams 25 and 28 both go to the Basílica.

Parque da Estrela

Parque da Estrela, one of the finest parks in Lisbon, is situated opposite the Basílica. There are well-designed and well-used play areas for children and lots of benches in the shade, as well as a pleasant open-air café. A spacious and elegant pavilion stands in the grounds and it is easy to imagine a band playing here on a sunny Sunday afternoon. On the north side of the park opposite the entrance is the old English Cemetery, where the writer Henry Fielding (1707–54), author of *The History of Tom Jones, A Foundling,* lies buried.

The Aqueduto das Águas Livres (*see page 58*) straddles the park, although directly behind the palace the water runs underground. A few ventilation towers identify the course of the water channel.

The opening times for the palace are short and it is advisable to enquire at the tourist office before visiting. Suburban trains from Rossio station to Sintra pass the edge of the park and the station nearest to the palace is Cruz da Pedra. Follow Rua de São Domingo de Benfica up to the palace. Alternatively, take the Metro to Sete Rios, walk along Estrada de Benfica, past the zoo on the right and then turn right into Rua de São Domingo de Benfica, which crosses the railway line and leads up to the palace.

Aqueduto das Aguas Livres

Aqueduto das Águas Livres. For centuries, summer water shortages have plagued Lisbon. The poor used to queue up by the few wells, many of which invariably dried up, and fights were regular occurrences. The better-off bought their water from the *aguadeiros*, the water-carriers, who would walk the streets carrying a water tank. For years plans had existed to build a conduit to bring water from the Águas Livres springs in the northwest of the town. King Manuel I studied the matter, later Sebastião even levied a tax to finance the construction of an aqueduct, but the town council squandered the proceeds on a state reception for Filipe II (Philip III of Spain) in 1619. The problem was not tackled again until 1729. This time a tax was levied on salt, olive oil, straw, wine and meat and the proceeds were invested in the construction work more or less straight away, before they could be spent on anything else. The work lasted well into the 19th century, but the valley crossing at Alcântara was completed in 1748 and the water then reached the town.

The huge undertaking was an engineering triumph for the main architects Custódio Vieira and Manuel de Maia, who had also worked on the reconstruction of the town after the 1755 earthquake. The main pipeline is 18km (10 miles) long, but the full length, including all the tributaries, is nearer 60km (35 miles). The water is carried solely by gravity along a gently falling incline, from a height of 180m (550ft) to the Lisbon plateau at 95m (300ft). For maintenance purposes, the water main has a diameter of about the height of a man. One branch of the pipeline also supplies Queluz and its castle (*see page 67*). About 10km (7 miles) from the city, the pipeline crosses a dam built by the Romans to create an artificial lake. Some old texts refer to a Roman conduit, which must have started at this lake.

The most difficult part of the whole project, and also the most impressive, is the crossing of the valley at Alcântara just outside the town gates. The aqueduct is supported by 35 arches and measures 941m (3,000ft) in total. For structural reasons, it does not follow the shortest route and is not a straight line. That it survived the earthquake is a tribute to the architects and engineers who worked on it. The tallest arch is 65m (200ft) high and 29m (90ft) wide. A footpath runs alongside the water course, which was used by farmers and traders for carrying their produce to Lisbon's markets, but in 1852 it was closed as it had become a favourite spot for suicide bids. In the Museu de Cidade, the municipal museum (*see page 61*), a room displays the 18th- and 19th-century drawings of the site, but sadly nothing remains of Alcântara's peaceful valley. The aqueduct crosses a network of busy roads and on the western side crosses a poor quarter of the city which is best avoided.

The aqueduct never fully met the needs of the growing city. By 1960, it supplied only 10 percent of the city's winter requirements and 1 percent during the summer, so despite the fact that it was still in excellent condition, it was closed down. The best view of the aqueduct is from Avenida Gulbenkian and also from the city motorway Viaduto Duarte Pacheco. The footpath across the valley has been re-opened in the past few years, but only on Saturday and Sunday from the beginning of June to the end of September (10am–12.30pm and 2–5.30pm). It can be reached from Calçada da Quintinha, off Rua Prof. Sousa da Câmara, which starts opposite the Amoreiras Shopping Centre (*see below*). Alternatively, take a number 2 bus from Cais de Sodré station or from the Rossio to the Campolide district where Calçada da Quintinha is situated.

Amoreiras Shopping Centre. The architect Tomás Taveira is responsible for this multi-storey development, which was completed in 1983. With its unusual colour combinations and extraordinary decorations, the post-modern design was, to say the least, controversial. Nevertheless, Taveira has become one of the most successful and most sought-after of Lisbon's architects. The interior design of this huge shopping complex is also striking – with 86,000 square metres (100,000 sq.yds) of shopping space, it has become Portugal's most fashionable place to shop. As the Amoreiras became such a pop-

Amoreiras Shopping Centre

ular place for *lisboetas* to stroll and browse, Baixa and Chiado have fallen out of favour with many shoppers and many people from the outlying areas have been drawn to this new shopping mecca, which is open from 10am to midnight. There is nothing specifically Portuguese about it and it could easily be a shopping mall in London, Paris or Hamburg. Nevertheless it is seen by many Portuguese people as an important step towards becoming Europeans, hence its anglicised name, the Shopping Centre. It can be reached by trams 24 and 25.

Azulejos, Mãe d'Agua das Amoreiras

A huge water tank with small ventilation towers can be seen just to the west. The aqueduct supplied this tank with water, but the main flow continued past the shopping mall and ended some 100m (320ft) further on in the Mãe d'Água das Amoreiras (*see below*).

Mãe d'Água das Amoreiras. This huge castle surrounded by water with a capacity of 5,500 cubic metres (12 million gallons) was designed by Carlos Mardel in 1752, but was not completed until 1834. The huge arches which lead up to the structure mark the end of the pipeline. The highlight is the arch which crosses Rua das Amoreiras and its design must surely have been inspired by the ancient triumphal arches. Inscriptions on both sides of the arch proclaim the completion in 1748 of the pipeline to Lisbon. In one of the arches stands the chapel of Nossa Senhora de Monserrate, but this is now usually locked. The castle itself is a simple structure with walls 5m (11ft) thick. The interior is an impressive sight. Inside a cavernous but ornamented hall, the water fell several yards into a basin. It is worth climbing on to the roof, not just for the view, but also to gain an insight into the workings of the pipeline.

The arch

Amoreira means mulberry tree in Portuguese and mulberry leaves are used to feed silk worms. It was here in the 18th century on a square on the edge of the town behind the water castle that Pombal planted the mulberry trees required by his silk factory. Some old, unremarkable buildings which date from about the same time can still be seen around the square; what is remarkable is that even in the middle of a major European capital city, a small corner of the past still exists almost unchanged.

In the Waterworks Museum

The Mãe d'Água is not open at regular times, but during the summer months it is sometimes used to stage concerts and other cultural events. Ask at the tourist office for more details.

For those who are still interested in the history of Lisbon's water supplies, the delightful EPAL museum is worth a visit. The Empresa Pública das Águas Livres or the **Municipal Waterworks Museum** is situated rather off the beaten track, halfway between Santa Apolónia station and the Madre de Deus monastery (*see page 61*) at

Rua de Alviela 12. Both are about 15 minutes' walk away but an alternative is to catch the 24 tram to Calçada de Santa Apolónia. Rua de Alviela is a side street off Calçada dos Barbadinhos, which starts opposite the tram stop. The museum documents the history of the city's water supplies with some unusual exhibits, which are generally clearly described. In an old pumping station, four enormous 19th-century steam engines, polished to a shine and still smelling of grease and coal, are imaginatively displayed. One of them has been reconditioned and can sometimes be seen working. Opening times: Tuesday to Saturday 10am–12.30pm and 2–5pm.

Museu da Cidade. The Municipal Museum stands in a rather forgotten corner of the Campo Grande, a long, narrow park in the north of the city. Close to a busy road junction, it has lost some of its appeal in recent years. It is housed in the Palácio Pimenta, which João V built in 1739 for his mistress, a nun by the name of Paula.

The Museu da Cidade is really a museum about Lisbon and its history. Many visitors to the city find that this museum has most to offer if it is included in the itinerary for the last day of their stay. They are then more likely to recognise the many pictures and models on display. The museum has recently been closed for renovation, but it is worth checking on progress at the tourist office. It can be reached by buses 7, 7a, 7b and 33 from Alvalade Metro station, although there is soon to be a new station, Campo Grande, when the Metro extension is completed.

Museu Militar (*see map on page 20/21*). The Military Museum, earlier known as the Artillery Museum, is housed in a building with an appropriate history. This site has been used for manufacturing weapons since 1640 and at times has been used as a weapons store for the army. The present building was constructed at the end of the 18th century and then extended at the end of the 19th century. The exhibits are displayed with an attention to detail expected from the military. In the courtyard is a collection of cannons and the exhibition rooms contain a comprehensive array of firearms.

For those not interested in weapons of war and military documents, the museum also has an extensive collection of 18th-century *azulejos* and paintings. Opening times: Tuesday to Saturday 10am–4pm, Sunday 11am–5pm. Closed Monday and holidays. The museum can be reached by taking the 24 tram.

★★ **Convento da Madre de Deus** and **Azulejo Museum.** The convent was founded in 1509 on the initiative of Manuel I's sister Leonor, but the earthquake in 1755 caused considerable damage. Only a small Manueline portal was left intact. The main portal was reconstructed in 1872 using the original plans.

Military Museum logo

Azulejo Museum entrance

The life of St Francis

Coronation of the Virgin

Entry to the church is via the museum. After the relatively modest exterior, the single-naved baroque interior, most of which dates from the latter half of the 18th century, is all the more surprising. The walls and ceilings are covered with *azulejos, talha dourada* (*see page 78*) and paintings. Yet despite the gleaming gold picture frames and altars, despite the ornate decorative work and an overwhelming sense of opulence, the effect is not oppressive or cluttered, in fact the atmosphere is more like a museum than a sacred building.

The blue-white *azulejos* show scenes from the life of St Francis and the life of St Clare. The semi-circular painting above the magnificent arch leading to the chancel shows the coronation of the Virgin Mary and the paintings in the altar room are among the oldest and date from the 16th century. The crypt is what remains of the original pre-earthquake church.

The cloister and other rooms in the convent now accommodate the Azulejo Museum which was founded with the assistance of the Gulbenkian Foundation in 1981. It is hoped that the museum will be extended in the coming years, for the collection at present, although fascinating, is not large. The original Madre de Deus tiles have been skilfully incorporated into the displays. The rooms around the cloister on the ground floor document how the tiles are made and also the development of tile painting, from its Moorish origins up to 1800. The second-floor cloister, which dates from Manueline times, is decorated with 18th-century tiles, including a fascinating pre-earthquake panorama of Lisbon, from Belém to the eastern edge of the city. A close study will reveal some long-gone tributaries of the Tejo, which were used to power tide mills. The old docks and wharves, the former royal palace and the Casa dos Bicos are all clearly visible as well.

One room on the first floor is devoted to 20th-century *azulejo* art and another is used for temporary exhibitions. A recent addition is a collection of tiles from the Netherlands. There is, as yet, no space for a fascinating series of pictures which tell the story of how a hatter found riches through sheer hard work. It is also possible to view the high chancel which is reached through the cloister. There was once a grille positioned in the wall, from where the nuns belonging to the strict Order of St Clare could attend the services unseen.

The museum café

Opening times: Tuesday to Sunday 10am–1pm and 2–5pm. Closed Monday and holidays. During the lunch break, visitors are allowed to sit in the cool shade of the inner courtyard and make use of the pleasant cafeteria. The convent can be reached by bus numbers 104 and 105 or else by the 24 tram, which involves getting out in Rua Madre de Deus and walking the last few hundred yards.

Excursions

Below are six recommended excursions into the city's hinterland. The first two head north of the Tejo, and the other two pass to the south of the river. Nearly all the places can be reached by tours operated from Lisbon by commercial bus companies and leaflets for them are usually available in most hotels. Some of the destinations can be reached using public transport.

Cais do Sodré station

1. Costa do Sol – ★★ Serra de Sintra

This tour is offered by all the sightseeing companies with only slight variations. But if the tour is split into sections,

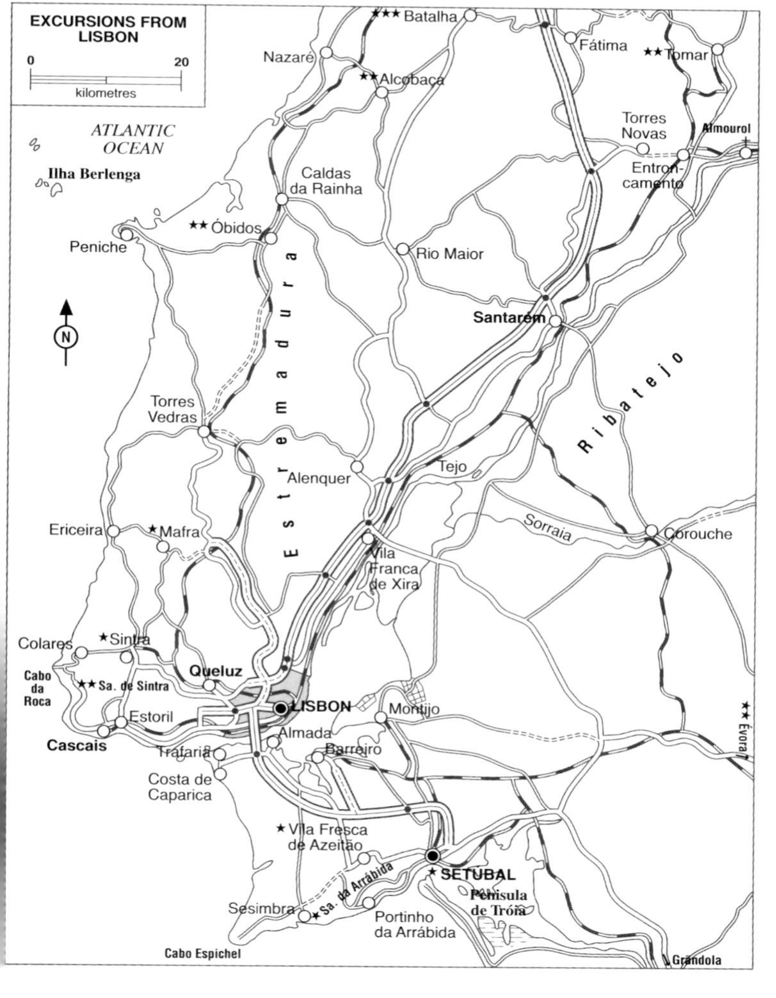

Fun on the beach

then take the local train from Cais do Sodré station to Estoril and Cascais. Another line goes to Sintra from Rossio station.

The Costa do Sol, which runs west along the coast from Lisbon, enjoys a mild climate. It has some beautiful sandy beaches and is becoming popular with wealthy Portuguese as well as tourists from abroad. In the summer, a constant stream of city dwellers arrives in search of rest and relaxation, but their cars can create congestion on the coastal roads. Although the climate and sandy beaches are very attractive, the seawater is no longer as clean as it used to be. Even the vast Atlantic is no protection against the constant onslaught of city pollution. Swimming is only advisable at a respectable distance from Lisbon, ie to the west of Estoril.

Take the suburban train or the busy N6 coastal road to Belém and Algés, well known for the **Aquário Vasco da Gama** (Tuesday to Sunday 10am–5pm, closed Monday and holidays) One of Marquês de Pombal's palaces lies a few hundred yards inland in a beautiful park and it is well worth a detour for its 16th-century *azulejos*.

This route follows the banks of the Tejo as it slowly widens and takes in Caxias, once famous for its prison for political detainees, Carcavelos, São Pedro de Estoril and finally **Estoril**. This one-time fishing village has become an international resort with the usual amenities: well-kept parks and villas, an excellent golf course, and a casino which offers a varied programme of events, including shows, films, concerts, plus the usual gambling games. The quality of water at the beaches is unreliable and a fisherman's life is no longer an easy one, yet Estoril has a certain Mediterranean-type charm all year round, with flowers, bushes, trees, attractive restaurants and other eating places. Open every night during the summer is the

Estoril park and casino

Feira do Artesanato, a craft fair, which is situated directly next to the casino.

Cascais, only 3km (2 miles) further on, has retained something of its past – it is still a busy fishing port, the local fishermen still supply the local restaurants and a walk through the town will reveal more than just rows of souvenir shops and discotheques.

Fisherman at Cascais

The town hall in Praça 5 de Outubro, formerly a stately home, contains some attractive *azulejos* depicting various saints. From here take Rua Marquês L Pancada to reach the church of Nossa Senhora de Assunção, which also has a number of tile pictures. They date from 1748 and show among other things the apocalypse. The citadel, with its commanding view of the bay, is not open to the public as it is still in the hands of the military. In the park nearby is the Museu Castro Guimarães, whose prehistoric finds are of more interest than the furniture and furnishings from the last century.

Follow Estrada da Boca do Inferno along the coast to the 'Mouth of Hell', the **Boca do Inferno**. Here the sea has partially hollowed out the rocky coastline and with a high tide and a reasonably strong breeze, it is easy to see how it acquired its name.

Boca do Inferno

The N247 coastal road now reaches the picturesque and popular Guincho beach. Beware! Car thefts are extremely common here. The beach, sand dunes and cliffs are a major attraction, but with the strong Atlantic tides, the seas can be very dangerous. It is therefore essential to heed the instructions of the lifeguards. If the red flag is flying, swimming is not allowed. There is a hotel close to the beach.

Guincho Beach

About 8km (5 miles) further north, take the N247 on the left to **Cabo da Roca**, the westernmost point of the continent of Europe. A little further along, the N247 passes Colares, once famous for its wine. From here the road leads further northwards to the beaches of Praia Grande, Praia de Maçãs and Azenhas do Mar. The N247 eventually goes to **Sintra**, but the route via the N375 is more picturesque. Keep right in Colares. A winding route leads through the mountains of ★★ **Serra de Sintra**. This mountainous landscape has immensely rich vegetation, benefiting from the southern sun and plenty of rain. At times when Lisbon is bathed in the scorching summer sun, Sintra will often be covered in clouds. As the original summer residence of the Portuguese kings, Sintra and the Serra soon attracted the Portuguese aristocracy. After Byron had written his romantic epic *Childe Harold's Pilgrimage* in praise of Sintra, it became a popular haunt for wealthy Britons in the late 19th and early 20th centuries. Many mansions, villas, country houses and *quintas* can be seen on the hillsides and in the town itself, and it is easy to believe that there are more foreigners living here than native Portuguese.

On the EN375 between Sintra and Colares is the ★ Parque de Monserrate with something like 3,000 plant varieties. A short distance further up the mountain on the left-hand side is the Palácio de Seteais, a five-star hotel with a commanding view of the coastline. The terrace is open to the public. The name of this palace, which was commissioned by a Dutch ambassador in the 18th century, means seven cries of terror (*sete ais*) which are said to have been uttered by the ambassador when presented with the bill. Its name is also connected with the Congress of Sintra (1808), a treaty which turned out to be a complete disaster for Portugal.

The Paço Real

The most popular attraction in **Sintra** itself is the ★ **Paço Real**, the royal palace at the lower end of town. Its characteristic features are immediately apparent: the two conical chimneys of the palace kitchens and the elegant twin windows that are reminiscent of Moorish times. The windows were booty, plundered in North Africa by João I, the founder of the Avis dynasty, who had them set into the palace in 1400. It was under King João I that the oldest surviving parts of the building were originally laid out, probably on the site of an existing Moorish castle. A hundred years later, under Manuel I, it was rebuilt in its present form. In spite of the crowds, a visit is well worthwhile but only possible as part of a conducted tour. (Open Monday to Sunday 10am–1pm and 2–5pm, closed Wednesday and holidays.)

Given the labyrinth of hallways, staircases and rooms, it is best to concentrate on the ★★ *azulejos*, of which the palace has many early examples. In the course of the tour, there is a fine view of the palace chapel from the balcony and what seems at first glance to be a beautiful old rug turns out to be a ceramic mosaic from the 15th century, similar to those found in Granada. The tiles of the Arabic Room and in the Dom Sebastião Room are said to date from around 1500. Some of these had already been produced in Portuguese workshops, others were still being imported from Seville. Almost all the rooms in the palace are decorated with tiles.

The palace's Heraldic Room

Apart from the precious *azulejos*, the visitor will find a number of other points of interest, including the impressive palace kitchen and several beautiful rooms each with a history of its own. In one, for example, Afonso VI, who was said to be mentally disturbed, was held prisoner by his brother from 1675 to the time of his death in 1683, even though he had already abdicated the crown in 1668. There is also the reading room or Hall of Magpies with 136 magpies on its wooden ceiling. They were painted on the orders of João I, each with a motto '*Por bem*' (I did it for the best) – his response once when reproached by ladies-in-waiting, who believed he had been having an affair. Finally, mention should be made of the finely painted ceilings in the ★ **Armorial Hall** and the Hall of Swans. Unfortunately the beautiful inner courtyards are not open to the general public.

Swan ceiling

The second royal palace in Sintra, the **Palácio da Pena**, is visible from afar thanks to its exposed position on the tip of the Serra. It is situated in the ★★ **Parque da Pena**, a series of gardens with a wide range of flora. The palace itself is a Portuguese version of the German 19th-century romantic castle. It was built in 1838 by Ferdinand von Saxe-Coburg-Gotha, the short-lived Prince Regent of Queen Maria II. He is also responsible for many other pioneering architectural projects of historical interest elsewhere in Portugal. It was his intention to create an architectural monument that would unite all previous artistic styles of Portugal and Germany. With the help of his master builder, Baron von Eschwege, he realised this plan. Gothic, Manueline, Renaissance and Rococo elements have been integrated in this new building, together with a two-storey cloister and a chapel with an altar by Chanterène, who was also responsible for the west portal of the Jerónimos Monastery in Belém.

The Palácio da Pena

There is a splendid ★ view along the coastline right out to the edge of Lisbon. Opening times: Tuesday to Sunday 10am–1pm and 2–5pm, closed Monday and holidays. Access from Sintra only by car or on foot.

You can enjoy the same magnificent view in the absence of any crowds or visitors by climbing the restored wall of the old Arabic castle. There is a car park on the left halfway along the road to the Palácio da Pena.

Approximately 1km (½ mile) away, below the Palácio da Pena, there is a road leading to the ★ **Convento dos Capuchos**, a Capuchin monastery founded in 1560. Some of its tiny cells have been hammered out of the rock and are lined with cork for insulation.

Beware! In the car parks near the tourist attractions, thieves have become skilled at breaking into vehicles.

When driving back to Lisbon, it is worth making a small detour via the **rococo palace** at Queluz. Turn into the EN117 on the edge of the town. Queluz railway station is on the Sintra-Lisbon line. This summer palace, built in 1750, has some attractive and richly decorated rooms, as well as carefully laid-out gardens. Opening times: Monday to Sunday 10am–5pm, closed Tuesday.

Queluz palace

2. ★★ *Mafra*

Mafra is situated 45km (30 miles) to the northwest of Lisbon and 20km (15 miles) to the north of Sintra, so travelling by car it would be quite easy to combine excursions 1 and 2. However, it is worth planning to stay one night in a hotel. From Sintra, take the EN9 to Mafra. Queluz (*see above*) can be visited on the way back, if preferred, in which case turn left in Pero Pinheiro on to the EN117 to reach Queluz via Belas. Buses operated by the Rodoviária Nacional run regularly from the Praça Marquês de Pombal to Mafra and Ericeira.

The palace at Mafra

When Portuguese people talk about **Mafra**, they are usually referring to the huge royal monastic palace beside the small town of the same name (pop. 5,000). In 1711 King João V promised to build a monastery if his wife produced a male heir. Finally the happy event occurred and in 1717 construction work began. In 1730 the church was consecrated, although completing the project lasted several decades, which is hardly surprising considering the enormous dimensions of the building – 40,000 sq m (48,000 sq yds) of roof, a facade 220m (700ft) long and nearly 900 rooms. In order to speed up the work, over 40,000 men were press-ganged into the service of the king, and then had to be guarded by soldiers. This massive undertaking is graphically described in a novel by the writer José Saramago.

Hoping to outdo the Spanish ruler's residence, El Escorial, João V funded this grand project with gold which was still flowing freely into the royal coffers, at least when the work started. The architect was Johann Friedrich Ludwig, who was born in Schwäbisch Hall in Germany and had completed his training in Italy. The building is therefore characterised by the Italian and German baroque styles and scarcely shows any Portuguese influence. The ground-plan consists of two large contiguous rectangles. At the centre of the first of these stands the Basílica. Its severe facade with two towers breaks up the extensive front elevation and is in harmony with the two corner pavilions. The interior of the church is more monumental than baroque in style. The decor is sparse and the combined use of different marbles creates an interesting play of colours. Particular mention should be made of some of the fine works of sculpture. The Italian master Alessandro Giusti started the Mafra School of sculpture here and one of the school's most celebrated pupils was Machado de Castro (*see page 57*).

Library

Part of the palace is still in use as a military barracks and it can therefore not be seen in its entirety, but any visitor to the long, monotonous corridors will hardly be surprised to learn that the royal family never in fact moved into this expensive edifice. Some rooms, however, provide an insight into the everyday life of the period, including the pharmacy, the hospital, the living quarters of the monks, and the kitchen. The **library**, very impressive at first sight, houses 30,000 volumes which include numerous valuable first editions. (Guided tours between 10am–5pm. Closed Tuesday.)

3. ★★ Óbidos – ★★ Alcobaça – ★★★ Batalha – Fátima – ★★ Tomar

Several coach companies in Lisbon offer day tours to these destinations. However, with so much to see and long distances to travel, one day is really not enough. If travelling by car, it is therefore well worth taking more time, perhaps considering a detour to the popular holiday resort of Nazaré on the coast. Generally the roads are good and well-signposted, but the section of road from Batalha to Tomar via Fatima is slower and has more bends than a cursory glance at the map might reveal. The total distance is approximately 350km (250 miles).

★★ **Óbidos** can be reached by rail from Rossio station and Tomar from Santa Apolónia station. In each case, the journey time is two hours. This small town has a long history thanks to its strategic location on the crest of a hill. There was a castle on this site in Moorish times, but the great attraction of Óbidos now is that it has retained its medieval charcacter. The whole of the town has been carefully restored and is protected by a preservation order.

Santa Maria church

Enter Óbidos from the south through a double town gate. This leads on to the main road which runs the whole length of the town. The Renaissance **church of Santa Maria** is situated in the town centre and is well worth a visit for its fine interior. The walls are covered with 17th-century tiles and the main altar, which dates from the Renaissance, depicts an unusual series of superbly painted scenes from the life of the Virgin Mary.

It is worthwhile making a detour down one of the pretty alleyways which adjoin the main street. At the far end is a castle which has been converted into a *pousada* (a state-

Óbidos castle and its walls

run hotel) and from here it is possible to climb on to the wall, which surrounds the whole town. From this commanding vantage point there are some fine views over the countryside as well as glimpses of this charming town, its narrow streets and alleyways.

★★ **Alcobaça.** The central focus of interest here is the **Cistercian monastery**. King Afonso Henriques is said to have vowed to build it when he captured Santaréms in 1147. In any event, the Cistercian order later rendered a very useful service by helping to spread Christian culture in the new Portuguese colonies.

The Cistercian monastery

The church dates from the 12th century and the monastery from the early 13th century. Changes were made later to the facade and only the portal is original. The windows, including the rose window, are Manueline, but in all other respects, baroque style predominates. All the more startling, therefore, is the effect of the interior. Here, in the largest church in the country, the unadorned Gothic style is enhanced by both the dimensions of the building and the way in which the light is directed on to the main altar. In the transept lie the carved ★★ **tombs** of King Pedro and his beloved Inés de Castro, who was murdered on the instructions of Pedro's father. Pedro later exacted a terrible revenge on the murderers and ordered the whole court to pay homage to the dead queen. The representation of the day of judgement on the tomb of Inés is particularly impressive. In one of the chapels other members of the House of Burgundy are buried.

The tomb of King Pedro

The monastery itself has some interesting features including the kitchen's enormous open hearths and the stream which provided the monks with a constant supply of fresh fish; the impressive vaulting in the refectory; and the cloister, where a second floor was added without upsetting the harmony of the whole. The well in the cloister is especially decorative.

★★★ **Batalha**. The House of Burgundy's monument to itself was the early Gothic Alcobaça monastery. For the next dynasty, the House of Avis, the monument was Batalha, a late Gothic-Manueline monastery. It was built following the Portuguese victory over the Castilians at the Battle of Aljubarrota in 1385. The statue on the forecourt dates from Salazar's time and is dedicated to the battle's hero, Nuno Alvarez Pereira.

The monastery at Batalha

Most of the monastery was completed by 1430 with the exception of the octagonal pantheon. However, interest in the project waned and so it was never finished. It is now known as Capelas Imperfeitas – the unfinished chapels.

The building has a unified appearance with strong horizontal and vertical elements. The style of the late-Gothic tracery and the ornamentation on the roof balustrades point to an English influence. Philippa of Lancaster, the wife of João I, brought in master builders from Britain. The features which deserve most attention include the portal on the church facade, the chapel dedicated to the founders, containing a combined tombstone for João I and Philippa, a magnificent well house in the Manueline cloister and the chapter house.

Fátima. On 13 May 1917 at the site of what is now the church, the Virgin Mary appeared before three shepherd children and asked them to pray for the peace of the world. She promised to appear before them on the 13th day of every month until October. The site soon became a centre of pilgrimage, although it was not acknowledged by the Catholic church until 1930. Today, Fátima and its large neo-classical basilica attracts pilgrims from all over the world, especially in the summer on each 13th day.

Picnic at Fátima

Despite the ugly new housing estates, the busy town of ★★ **Tomar** (pop. 15,000) has managed to preserve its charming centre which sits astride the Rio Nabão. It is an ideal spot for a relaxing stroll with a number of places of interest including a waterwheel modelled on an old Arabic design, some 16th-century barns that were used as mills and in the heart of the town a 15th-century synagogue. The church of São João Baptista has a rather squat appearance despite its beautiful Manueline portal.

Tomar on the Nabão

The Convent of the Order of Christ is situated on the top of the hill which dominates Tomar, but about halfway up this hill stands one of the most beautiful Renaissance buildings in the country, the little church of ★ **Nossa Senhora da Conceição**. Despite its plain exterior, it is well worth a look inside. The side aisles of this triple-naved church are divided by Corinthian pillars topped by decorated barrel vaulting. The walls are divided up by pilasters and triangular gables and the small dome has a coffered ceiling. An elegant spiral staircase leads up to the roof terrace which provides a fine view of the town and the convent. Ask for the keys at the tourist office in Avenida Cândido Madureira.

★★ **The Convent of the Order of Christ**. Originally, the convent (12th-17th century) was the seat of the Knights Templar. Their order was suppressed in 1312 by Pope Clemens II on the initiative of the French King Phillip the Fair. The Portuguese kings, however, were not in favour of the suppression, as the knights had been their stalwart supporters in the battle against the Arabs. The solution was quite simple: the Order of the Knights Templar changed its name to the Order of Christ and their headquarters remained in Tomar.

Detail on the convent

The fortified walls have only partially survived. They date back to the time of the Templars, as does the Charola, the old sixteen-sided Templar chapel from which the knights drew their spiritual strength. The entrance to the

The Claustro do Cemitério

A vaulted ceiling inside the convent

The Manueline window

chapel is by a splendid ★ **Manueline portal** and a circular aisle surrounds a two-storeyed octagon containing the high altar. There is a complex vaulting structure linking the altar room with the exterior walls.

Of the seven cloisters in the convent, the ★ **Claustro do Cemitério** is probably the highlight – in fact, it is one of the most beautiful Gothic cloisters in the entire country. Another impressive cloister, and a fine example of the Renaissance, is the ★ **Claustro dos Felipes**, which dates from the time of Spanish rule, hence its name. Finally, mention should be made of an exquisite feature on the on the west face of the church: the ★ **Manueline window** reveals the Manueline style at its most extravagant with ornamental corals, ships' ropes, and anchors. Further Manueline decoration can be found on one of the towers, which has a huge belt wrapped around it.

4. Costa da Caparica

Costa da Caparica on the south bank of the Tejo has become the most popular beach for the *lisboetas*. The traffic jams which form by the Ponte 25 de Abril in the mornings as the sun seekers leave the city and in the evenings when they return, speak for themselves. Try to avoid the bridge on Sunday evenings when the weekend trippers are returning en masse.

To get to the Costa da Caparica beach take the urban motorway to the Tejo bridge and follow the road signs. Even though the beach extends for 15km (10 miles), there still does not seem to be enough room. The further away from the city, the bigger the crowds. It is possible to get there by public transport. First take the train to Belém and cross the river to Trafaria by ferry. Catch a bus to Caparica and then take the railway along the coast. It seems complicated but is really quite simple.

5. Sesimbra – ★ Serra da Arrábida – ★ Setúbal

This tour is best undertaken by car, although some sections of it may be included in organised coach tours.

Cross to the south by the Tejo bridge and leave the motorway at the second exit. Take the EN378 to Santana, bear right and follow signs to Cabo Espichel. There is often a strong breeze blowing on to the promontory, and here stands a church, which houses an image of the Virgin found by a fisherman who was guided by its incandescence. Two long arcaded wings for accommodating pilgrims project forward from the church.

Return to Santana and head further south to **Sesimbra** (pop. 8,500). A Moorish castle looks down on this fishing village, now a mecca for tourists and hemmed in by holiday developments.

Return again to Santana and this time follow the EN379 to the right and then, before reaching Aldeia dos Irmãos, turn onto the EN379-1. This leads through the delightful ★ Serra da Arrábida. The Serra is now a nature reserve and parts of it are closed to visitors to protect some threatened plant species. A footpath which leads back almost as far as Sesimbra begins near the point where the EN379-1 turns to the east.

On the right, a country road leads to the small resort of Portinho de Arrábida. It is very popular in the summer months and parking can be a problem. The EN379-1 continues through attractive but hilly terrain as far as ★ **Setúbal** (pop. 78,000). This old port has faced a number of problems as its traditional industries have had difficulty adjusting to change. The old town with its traffic-free shopping streets is ideal for browsing and a good place to buy shoes. The main sights, the Igreja de Jesús and the neighbouring Museu da Cidade (Town Museum) are situated in Avenida 22 de Dezembro, one of the town's main thoroughfares.

Work on the ★ **Igreja de Jesús** was started by Boytac in 1491 during the reign of King João II but not finished until Manuel I came to the throne. It is regarded as one of the first Manueline churches. Look out for the portal on the south side and the large, elegant window in the chancel a little further to the right. The best view of the interior is from the balcony and it is the six twisted pillars which will undoubtedly attract the eye.

The pictures of the so-called Master of the Altar of Setúbal used to decorate the church, but these portrayals of the saints, which originated around 1500, are now on display in the Town Museum. The museum also houses archaeological finds, a golden Gothic processional cross and collections of coins, books and *azulejos*. Opening times: Tuesday to Sunday 9am–12.30pm and 2–5.30pm. Closed Monday and holidays.

Beach near Sesimbra

Sesimbra surfer

Fountain in Setúbal

Start the return journey via the EN10 to **Vila Fresca de Azeitão.** In the village, hidden by a wall, is the ★ Quinta da Bacalhoa, a 15th-century villa now in private hands, but the garden may be visited. Labyrinthine clipped box hedges are hemmed in by 16th-century tiles, some depicting the rape of Europa and some with geometric patterns. The house's pretty loggia can be seen from the garden. Opening times: Monday to Saturday 1–5pm.

About 1km (½ mile) further on to the left is the Estalagem de Quinta das Torres, also a summer villa, but built in Renaissance style with some fine 16th-century Italian tile pictures depicting the burning of Troy and the death of Dido. Follow the EN10 as far as the Lisbon motorway.

Main square, Évora

6. ★★ Évora

The old provincial capital of Évora (pop. 45,000) is situated on the gentle slope of a wide hill on the Alentjan plain. It is now very firmly on the tourist map of Portugal and the local hoteliers and restaurateurs have taken advantage of the town's popularity. But it is not just the tourists who are attracted to Évora; transactions at the market and the local government offices draw in the farmers and country-dwellers, and the cafés and Praça do Giraldo always look busy.

This walled town has managed to avoid many urban excesses, so a morning walking the clean, cobbled streets, admiring the arches and arcades, the whitewashed *palácios* and Renaissance fountains is certainly time well spent.

The town walls to the north and the west date from medieval times. A 15th-century aqueduct crosses the wall to bring water from a distance of 18km (10 miles). The rest of the town's fortifications date from the 17th century, although a small section of the wall is Roman.

Ruins of the royal palace

The ruins of a Manueline **royal palace** with some fine examples of double windows can be seen in the park (Jardim Público) to the south of the city. On the road back to the town centre stands the Igreja de São Francisco, a 15th-century church with a Manueline portal and a macabre **Bone Chapel** (Casa dos Ossas). Most of the other sights are close to Praça do Giraldo, the picturesque main square, which is surrounded by arcaded old houses. A magnificent Renaissance fountain stands in the middle of the square and to the north is Santo Antão, a 16th-century church. Rua 5 de Outubro to the right or one of the other small lanes leads up to the ★★ **Sé**. Évora's cathedral is a mixture of Romanesque and Gothic features and is certainly Portugal's best example of ecclesiastical architecture from this period. Rugged and squat in appearance with battlements, a spiked tower and a Romanesque belfry, it has a row of stern-looking apostles above the porch. The baroque choir was remodelled in the 18th century and

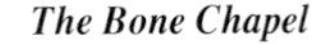

The Bone Chapel

The Temple of Diana

stands out from the characteristically Romanesque nave. The 15th-century statue of Nossa Senhora da Ó, a pregnant Mary, is unusual, as is the ★★ **Ivory Madonna** in the Treasury. The cloister is also worth a visit.

To the left of the cathedral stands the old Bishop's Palace, which now houses the Museu Regional. It displays paintings from the 15th to 17th centuries and Roman and medieval sculptures, as well as some interesting tapestries from Arraiolos, a village 30km (20 miles) north of Évora. Opposite the museum is the ★ **Temple of Diana.** Believed to have been built in the 1st century, the temple has survived in good condition for so long because it was covered over, having fulfilled a number of different functions over the centuries, including a period as the municipal slaughterhouse. But in 1870 it was finally opened up to the elements and now its fluted pillars rise majestically into the sky.

Excavations under the town hall unearthed a *frigidarium*, a cold water bath dating from Roman times. The town boasts many other places of interest including more fine churches, monasteries, palaces and old town houses. Several of the churches – Espirito Santo and São Maurede, for example – have beautiful examples of tile 'carpets' on their walls (*see page 27*). Évora has a history stretching back many centuries and evidence of its distinguished past can appear around any corner.

The journey to Évora from Lisbon takes about three hours, whether on an organised coach tour or by ferry and train from the Estação Marítima, the station to the east of Terreiro do Paço. Times of ferries to Barreiro station on the south bank of the Tejo are shown on the timetable and the price of the ticket includes the ferry crossing.

The Tejo car ferry

Art History

During the 1980s, Roman remains were found in Rua Augusta in Baixa and also among the Castelo de São Jorge fortifications, but the results of these excavations are not yet on display to the public.

Much more was bequeathed to the city by the Arabs. Any words beginning with 'al-' indicate Arab origins, such as Alcântara, the name of a Lisbon district, or *alface*, a green salad. The latter has become a nickname for the peo-ple of Lisbon, *alfacinhas* or 'salad eaters', on account of :heir predilection for green salads. As is clear from their ıames, both Alfama and Mouraria, the poor quarters on :he edge of Baixa, go back to the days of the Arab occu-ɔation. Around the middle of the 12th century, work started ɔn the Sé, the predominantly Romanesque cathedral. The ;ite for the new church had previously been occupied by he Arab mosque.

Portugal's glory days are long gone, but much of what /ou see in Lisbon reflects its golden past. A portrait of Ienry the Navigator which probably bears a close simi-arity to the energetic prince can be seen on the great polyp-ych by court painter Nuño Gonçalves. This altarpiece, *'he Adoration of St Vincent*, is on display in the Museu Nacional de Arte Antiga (*see page 54*) and is certainly one of Portugal's most significant works of art. The city's coat of arms is also dedicated to St Vincent, the city's patron aint. According to legend, the body of Vincent, who had een martyred in Spain in 287, was first thrown onto a field vhere two ravens guarded it. The body was then cast into he sea, where the ravens continued to keep guard over t – the scene which the coat of arms depicts. His body was ater washed up near the port of Sagres on the Algarve oast and the remains of the saint are now preserved in shrine in Lisbon's cathedral. Avila, in Spain, however, laims to have Vincent's tomb.

In Portugese culture, fine building is the dominant art. heritage of empire, it lives on in castles and churches round the world; you'll see it in the variety of styles that dorn Lisbon, from medieval to Manueline, Mannerist ɔ neo-classical and post-modern. The new riches which ccrued during the 15th and 16th century were invested in ıe district of Belém. The splendid palace that King Ianuel I (1495–1521) built was destroyed in the 1755 arthquake. Manuel, sometimes referred to as Manuel the ortunate, was on the Portuguese throne when the coun-y's reputation was at its zenith. He gave his name to Por-ıgal's only distinct architectural style, the Manueline. The Ianueline style is essentially lavish surface decoration, 'ith a preoccupation for the nautical world with cables nd knots and the art of distant lands. However, the most

A street in Alfama
Opposite: Cathedral chapel

Praça do Comércio

Manueline palace ruins, Évora

significant works of the Manueline style do demonstrat a variation in structural elements and a passion for twiste piers. Manueline influences can be seen in the art of th goldsmith, and the finest example of this kind of work i the famous Monstrance of Belém, created for the Jerón imos Monastery, probably by playwright Gil Vicent (1465–1536). The Monstrance is on display in the Muse de Arte Antiga (*see page 54*).

Drama also flourished during the 'Golden Years' of th discoveries. Gil Vicente wrote many plays for the cour – *comédias* (comedies), *farças* (farces) and *moralidade* (morality plays) and he is now regarded as the founde of Portuguese theatre. But as a sharp-eyed and critical ob server of his times, he incurred the displeasure of his pa trons and was imprisoned by the Inquisition prior to hi death. The best-known medieval poet is Luís de Camõe (1525–1580), who is said to have written *The Lusiads*, fo which he is now revered as Portugal's national poet. Thi epic tale glorified the heroic deeds of his fellow-coun trymen on their voyages of discovery. Camões' death o 10 June is now commemorated in one of Portugal's fou national holidays.

São Roque, interior; São Vincente de Fora, facade

During the unhappy period of Spanish rule, the Man nerist style, which had its origins in Italy, dominated Por tuguese art and architecture. The principal examples i Lisbon are in the church of São Roque (*Route 3*) and Sã Vicente de Fora (*Route 2*).

Nowhere is royalty's love of pomp and splendour bet ter reflected than in the monastery-palace at Mafra, buil between 1717 and 1735 by 45,000 workmen to celebrat the birth of a child to King João V. The same king wa responsible for the ambitious construction of the Lisbo Aqueduct of Free Waters, which survived the great earth quake of 1755 and is still largely intact.

Gold plundered from Brazil was used not only to fun mammoth building projects, but also to decorate churche with *talha dourada* or gilt carving in Portuguese baroqu style. An example is the interior of the church of Madr de Deus (*see pages 61–2*). Interiors were further enriche by 'tapestries' of painted tiles known as *azulejos* (*see pag 80*). There are not a large number of baroque building in Lisbon itself, but the palace of Queluz, 5km (3 miles northwest of Lisbon, is the finest example of late-baroqu architecture in Portugal.

Pombal had Baixa redesigned

After the great earthquake, the enlightened Marquês d Pombal ordered the demolition and removal of any re maining buildings and employed the great architects o the day to redesign Baixa, the lower town, in a neat geo metric grid. He insisted that the streets in the town cen tre were to be for the benefit of the merchants an craftsmen and not the aristocracy. At the time, the street had been wider than seemed necessary, so there was now space for pavements and with the installation of a sewerage system, Lisbon became a model for contemporary town-planners.

In the 19th century, the smarter side of Lisbon extended north from Baixa. Wide, elegant boulevards such as the Avenida da Liberdade were built and parks, including the Botanical Gardens, were designed. As the city evolved during the 19th century, the authorities at least retained some of Pombal's guiding principles by adhering to a plan with all the necessary domestic and social amenities. In recent years many of the fine town houses in the Avenida da Liberdade and nearby streets have given way to modern monstrosities. However, a few of these beautiful houses have been preserved and convey some of the charm of 19th-century residential architecture. Not so striking, but no less pretty, are the city's iron kiosks, some of which still fulfil their original function.

19th-century house

Iron kiosk

Unaffected by the turbulent political situation in the early years of the 20th century, the city continued to expand. The Avenida da Liberdade was enhanced by the Parque Eduardo VII and more wide avenues, the Avenidas Novas, were built in the north of Lisbon. In this part of the city, three distinct architectural styles can be detected: firstly there are the buildings from the turn of the century, although the same style was in use well into the 1920s; secondly there is the so-called Modernist style of the 1930s, which fitted in with the austerity of the Salazar regime; and thirdly the modern concrete blocks of the 1970s and 1980s which, on the whole, were constructed without any thought as to how they might blend in with their surroundings.

During the Salazar regime, the need for impressive projects led to the construction of huge squares and buildings, particularly in the north of the city and in Belém (Praça do Império (*Route 6*). Many grand monuments were built, particularly in the centre of the new squares (Praça de Londres, Alameda de Afonso Henriques, *Route 5*). New housing developments were mainly built on the northwest outskirts of the city, near the Parque de Monsanto and in the northeast between the river and the airport, but Bairro do Arco Cego ((*Route 5*) is the best example of how this architectural style put the church and the school at the heart of the community.

Designed and built in 1966 by a team of American engineers, the ambitious Tejo bridge project was completed and named the Salazar Bridge, but it has subsequently been renamed the Ponte 25 de Abril. In addition to the new bridges and roads, the most eye-catching symbols of modern Lisbon are the glass towers of the Amoreiras, a shopping centre beloved of the city's youth.

Ponte 25 de Abril

Tile restoring

Azulejos

Portugal is famous for its 'tile tapestries', pictures, designs, even whole house fronts made up of decorative tiles (*azulejos*). The usual colour combination is blue on a white background. The manufacturing skills are Persian in origin and came to Spain with the Arabs; influenced by the palace at Granada, João II and Manuel I had Spanish tiles made by Moorish craftsmen shipped to Portugal.

The tiles were first combined to form complex geometric patterns. During the Italian Renaissance, the technique known as *majolica* was developed. Expansive organic drawing replaced the geometric shapes, and themes from Greek mythology appeared on Renaissance panels. The finest example is at the Vila Fresca de Azeitão (*see page 74*). The tiles themselves either came from abroad or were made in Portugal under the direction of Flemish craftsmen. The Palácio Fronteira on the edge of the city was built in the spirit of the Renaissance and the gardens contain a lavish collection of 17th-century designs. The Portuguese artists' love of ornamentation and colour derives from the encounters of the master mariners with the Far East during the voyages of discovery. The patterns of Indian silks and the pure blue of Chinese porcelains were a source of inspiration.

Typical Portugese tiles

While the panels by Francisco de Matos (1578) in the aisle of the Chapel of São Roque (*see page 29*) are masterpieces of Mannerist art, impressive pictorial works covering whole walls, set alongside the motifs associated with *talha dourada*, were typical of the baroque period (end of the 17th/beginning of the 18th century). *Azulejos* not only provided a decorative finish, enriching churches and secular buildings at a low cost, but offered protection against the elements. In the years following the Napoleonic invasion and the liberal revolution, *azulejos* gained even greater popularity and were used as facades for town houses and business premises, particularly bakeries and taverns. A good example of such a facade can be seen on the Cervejaria da Trinidade (*see page 29*).

At the beginning of the 20th century, there were two distinct styles in circulation: art nouveau and art deco mimicked popular designs from northern Europe, while the national style chose scenes from everyday life and monuments portrayed as on a postcard. After 1940, the Estado Novo architecture found little use for *azulejos*, but they have recently become fashionable again and are greatly admired. This revival of interest in *azulejos* has led to the opening of a small museum in the convent of Madre de Deus (*see page 62*). Three new Metro stations in the northwest of the city have been decorated with *azulejos* by modern artists and it is worth seeking out these contemporary applications of the distinctive Portuguese tile.

Cervejaria da Trinidade

Fado illustrated in tile

Fado and Saudade

Fado is to Portugal what *flamenco* is to Spain, but beyond that tenuous link there is not much similarity. The word *fado* derives from the Latin and means quite simply 'fate'. The music, nearly always in a minor key, expresses melancholy and seems to have originated in Lisbon in the latter part of the 18th century as a synthesis of several influences including the medieval troubadour, Moorish music and the songs of the Brazilian *mestizos*. There are conflicting views on what *fado* should be. 'An urban folk song and totally genuine,' writes Gallop who has written an account of 20th-century Portuguese folk music. Another musical historian Lopes Graça, however, dismisses it as commercial and artificial.

Nowadays *fado* can be heard mostly in expensive restaurants, but it was originally performed in bars by a *fadista* with a guitar accompaniment. Lisbon's *fado* compares with ballad-style folk songs and can be cheerful, but is more often mournful, with a fatalistic theme. The words are often strings of clichés and the subject matter is life, love, *saudade* or *fado* itself.

Saudade is a difficult word to translate as there is no word for it in any other language: longing, perhaps, homesickness, the feeling of missing someone or something, an ache in the soul. It reflects the national character of the Portuguese and is the sentiment most deeply expressed in the *fado*.

Fado houses, or *adega tipica* as they are sometimes known, go to great lengths to attract customers. Find a *tasca* or a small bar in Bairro Alto for authentic, improvised *fado*, sung for a Portuguese audience, rather than being drawn into an artificial setting devised purely for tourists, such as is often found in Alfama.

Music shop, Chiado

Performing fado

Food and Drink

Portuguese and Spanish cooking have much in common as 'country cooking' predominates. Simple ingredients are used to create tasty meals without frills. Those who give the international dishes a miss and seek out a small restaurant or *tasca* will find they can eat very cheaply, thereby getting to know the pleasures of simple Portuguese food and saving money. Lunch is usually served from noon onwards, while evening meals are served from 7.30pm.

The Portuguese are a sea-faring nation and, not surprisingly, fish *(peixe)* and seafood *(mariscos)* nearly always feature on the menu. While *caldeirada* is a fish stew with potatoes, *arroz da marisco* is a Portuguese version of paella, combining seafood with rice.

Meat is sometimes mixed with mussels *(à alentejana)*. Grilled sardines *(sardinhas)* are fatty but cheap and very tasty. Other fish dishes include *linguado* (sole), *cherne* (perch), *enguia* (eel), *robalo* (sea bass), *atum* (tuna) and *lulas* (squid). But a true Portuguese meal would not be complete without *bacalhau*. Dried cod is Portugal's favourite fish, but there are said to be 365 different ways of cooking it.

A typical fish dish
Opposite: a break from the kitchen chores

In the *carne* (meat) section of the menu, there will always be *bife* (steak), *boi* or *vaca* (beef), *porco* (pork) and *frango* (chicken). Other meat dishes are *borrego* (lamb) and *cabrito* (kid). *Cozido à portuguesa* is a casserole of various meats and sausages served with rice and a variety of vegetables.

Vegetables are usually added to soups, but sometimes *ervilhas* (peas), *cenouras* (carrots), *pimentos* (peppers), *congumelos* (mushrooms), *alface* (lettuce) or *salada mista* (mixed salad) are served as accompaniments.

Desserts are given a special status in Portugal and there is invariably a choice between fruit, cheese, ice-cream and cakes. *Maçãs* (apples) are eaten raw or in a mixed salad *(salada da frutas)*, with either *pêras* (pears), *morangas* (strawberries), *melões* (melons), *laranjas* (oranges), *pêssegos* (peaches) or *uvas* (grapes). There are of course *gelado* or *sorveto* (ice creams), *bolo* or *tarta* (cakes) and *doces* (sweetmeats), but the latter are often too sweet for many palates. One of the best cheeses, *queijo daserra*, comes from the hilly rural areas.

Fresh peaches

The *vinho da casa* or house wine is usually red *(tinto)*, rarely white *(branco)*. Northern Portugal produces *vinho verde* or green wine, which is a refreshing, light wine, while *dão* and *douro* are red wines produced on the banks of Portugal's main rivers. Both of these wines compare favourably with any French or Italian red.

Wine selection

Cerveja (beer) usually comes bottled, while for drivers or teetotallers, the choice is between *água mineral* or fruit

Café Brasilia

juices, for example *sumo de maça* (apple juice) or *sumo de laranja* (orange juice).

After coffee, *bagaço* is a popular spirit, a type of eau-de-vie or brandy. Another popular but more expensive brandy is *aguardente velha*. For a strong expresso coffee, ask for *uma bica*, but if milk is required, then order *café com leite*. *Um galão* is an expresso coffee but diluted with milk.

Restaurants

The following is a selection of restaurants in the expensive and medium price categories:

$$$

Tágide, Largo da Academia, Nacional de Belas Artes 18 (traditional and expensive, but with a fine view of the city and the river); **Tavares Rico**, Rua da Misericórdia 37 (excellent reputation, but expensive); **Casa da Comida**, Travessa das Amoreiras 1 (elegant decor with imaginative menu, expensive).

$$

Conventual, Praça de Flores 45; **O Faz Figura**, Rua do Paráiso 15b (superb view); **O Polícia**, Rua Marquês Sá da Bandeira 112; **Múni**, Rua dos 115; **Brasuca**, Rua J Pereira da Rosa (Brazilian cuisine); **Trindade**, Rua Nova da Trindade (a beer hall with 19th-century *azulejos*, cool in the summer).

The Vienna Café

The street which offers the widest selection of eating places is Rua das Portas de Santo Antão, near Praça dos Restauradores. There are some good restaurants here, but they are geared towards tourists. Small restaurants or *tascas* can usually be found in the older districts of Lisbon, such as Bairro Alto or in the streets near the station. Many such *tascas* are closed at the weekend.

Outdoor dining

Shopping and souvenirs

Fashionable shops are not only to be found in the Baixa and Chiado districts; Avenida da Roma and Avenida Liberdade are also excellent centres for high-quality, if sometimes rather expensive, goods. There are small malls throughout the city, a high-class one at the Ritz, and an enormous one at Amoreiras.

All the latest fashion

Ceramics, tiles
Hand-painted ceramics which vary in colour and pattern are typical souvenirs.
Santa Ana, Rua do Alecrim 91–97. Classical ceramics and *azulejos*, all hand-painted.
Fábrica de Céramica Viúva Lamego, Largo do Intendente 25. This quaint shop has some pottery and a wide choice of tiles.
Alberquerque & Sousa lda, Rua do Dom Pedro V 66–72. Beautiful antique tiles from the 17th–20th centuries.

Jewellery
Silver and gold are good value in Lisbon and making filigree jewellery is a Portuguese craft.
Ouriversaria Aliança, Rua Garrett 50 is a delightful shop.
Eloy de Jesus, Rua Garrett 45. Beautiful, high-quality silver filigree.
Sarmento, Rua Aurea 251. Good selection of traditional filigree in both silver and gold.
Torres, Rua Aurea 202, 253, 255; and Rua Augusta 257. Items both antique and modern.

Bead seller

Embroidery, lace
Embroidered table cloths, usually from the north or Madeira, make good souvenirs.
Casa Regional da Ilha Verde, Rua Paiva de Andrada 4. A beautiful selection of hand-made items, primarily from the Azores.
Madeira Gobelins, Rua Castilho 40. Lots of embroidered works in a rather touristy setting.

Arrailos rugs
Arraiolos rugs from Arraiolos in the Alentejo are beautifully woven.
Casa Quintão, Rua Ivens 30. Off Rua Garrett in Chiada. This is one of the best known stores of its kind.
Casa dos Tapetes de Arraiolos, Rua do Imprensa Nacional 166E. Beautiful, customised rugs.

Basketware is another good example of Portuguese craftwork. Other popular presents are likely to be sweet wines such as port and Moscatel de Setúbal.

Souvenirs

SUL-PONTE
ESTORIL
Parque Municipal
Torre de Belém
MONIZ
SIO
S. Jorge

Getting There

By Air

TAP Air Portugal is the national carrier. The city is also served by some 20 other airlines including British Airways and TWA, with offices in Avenida da Liberade. Look out for cheap deals, late bookings and charter flights. Many tour operators provide packages. UK operators include Caravela Tours, Time Off and Travelscene. US operators often include Lisbon in combined tours of Portugal and Spain.

Lisbon's Portela airport is situated 13km (8 miles) north of the city centre. The green and white buses of the Linha Verde, the municipal bus company, operate between the airport, the city centre and the Santa Apolónia station.

TAP-Air Portugal information and reservations: Praça Marquês de Pombal 3, tel: 53 88 52.

Lisbon airport
Opposite: pointing the way

By Train

Rail travel is likely to be more expensive than flying, but there are deals for extensive travel and for under-26s.

The main rail connections are through the Gare d'Austerlitz in Paris and take up to two and a half days. The Sud Express runs to the west of the Pyrenees, changing trains at Hendaye/Irun, and *couchettes* should be booked. A more luxurious way to travel would be on the Talgo direct to Madrid, changing on to the Lisboa Express. International trains arrive at the Santa Apolónia station, from where the Linha Verde buses run to the city centre.

Bus

From the UK: The National Express bus company runs Eurolines to Lisbon on Tuesday and Saturday from Victoria Coach Station in London. Although cheap, they may not be as cheap as a charter flight. The journey takes under 48 hours. Tickets tend to be open, so make sure you book a seat for coming back. In Lisbon: Intercentro, Avenida Casal Ribiero 16.

Traffic jam

By Car

From Calais it is just over 1,100 miles to Lisbon and the journey takes about three days. The twice-weekly ferry from Plymouth to Santander, northern Spain, takes 24 hours, then there is a couple of days of leisurely driving. The following border posts between Spain and Portugal are open 24 hours: Valença do Minho, Vilar Formoso, Caia (near Elvas).

Fuel prices are similar to those in Britain and lead-free fuel (*gasolina sem chumbo*) is readily available. Nationality plates must be displayed, and an international Green Card insurance certificate is obligatory. .

Getting Around

Cars and car rental

Unless it is absolutely unavoidable, do not venture into Lisbon on four wheels. Firstly, cars with foreign registration plates are an obvious target for thieves. Hire cars are also at risk as they can be quickly identified. Secondly, Portuguese drivers and particularly those from Lisbon are aggressive and often dangerous. Thirdly, traffic jams are commonplace during busy periods. If the journey to Lisbon has to be by car, leave it in a garage on arrival or at least park it in a busy, well-lit spot. Never leave anything valuable in the car.

Car rental is relatively expensive, but it is probably inevitable when visiting otherwise inaccessible destinations, such as the Serra da Arrábida (*see page 73*). Drivers have to be at least 21 years old and must produce their driving licence when making the booking. Credit cards are usually accepted in payment. Addresses of car rental companies and prices are available at the airport and in most hotels. During the summer, it is advisable to arrange car rentals well in advance.

Taxi stand in Baixa

Taxis

As a general rule, Lisbon's black and green taxis are reasonably priced, but it is often difficult to find one for hire during busy periods. Taxis available for hire can be recognised either by the sign *livre* or a green light on the front windscreen. The two green lights on the roof are to indicate the tariff. A green light next to the sign denotes daytime tariff, while two green lights denote night-time tariff. Inside the city boundaries the meter indicates the fare, but out of town the fare is calculated according to the number of kilometres travelled. A problem sometimes arises because the taxi meter has not been adjusted to include the latest price rise. The driver then adds a supplement to the price shown on the meter. Provided the traffic is not too heavy, one way to see the sights is to hire a taxi for, say, two hours, at an agreed price.

Tejo car ferry

Sightseeing tours

An organised sightseeing tour is ideal for the older visitor and such a tour will cover all the main sights. The tourist information centres and most hotels will provide details of the tour operators.

Trains and ferries

Many of the shorter excursions can be made by local trains or ferries, or a combination of the two. Journey times, stations, etc for the excursions in this guide are given where appropriate.

Metro

The Metro is limited, and like all underground systems it is easy to follow. It has 26 stops and just two lines, both of which start from Rossio – one goes to the northeast of the city, the other to the northwest. Work is going ahead, in stages, to extend the network with five more stations on three lines: Line 1 Rato to Campo Grande; Line 2 Baixa-Chiado to Pontinha; Line 3 Cais de Sodré to Pontinha. The scheme is scheduled for completion sometime in 1995.

Trains run from 6.30am to 1am. Passengers are warned of the increased risk of pickpockets at busy times.

Metro sign

Buses, trams and elevadores

These transport services are all run by the municipal Carris company.

Paragem means stop. When the word on the stop is shown in capitals, PARAGEM, then all trams stop there. When the word is written in small letters with a series of numbers, then it is a bus stop only for the bus routes shown. Buses cover the whole city, but only during the day. At night and at weekends, many services stop or run less frequently.

The trams are an important tourist attraction and are an ideal means of transport for the many hilly routes. Timetables are only shown at the main stops and some routes do not operate at weekends. Passengers are expected to wait in queues for buses, trams and taxis and should give a hand signal to stop a bus or a tram.

Funicular railway

Lisbon has three funicular railways or *elevadores* and one unusual lift. They are mentioned in more detail in the appropriate routes.

It is more economical to buy a ten or twenty ticket booklet in advance. The tickets can be used on all forms of municipal transport within the city. A day ticket is also good value, as is the tourist pass, but the latter can be used on the Metro as well and can be purchased for four or seven days. They may all be purchased in advance at the Cais do Sodré or Santa Apolónia stations, the Carmo *elevador* or by the Parque Eduardo VII in Avenida Sidónio Pais. The tourist passes and a plan of the whole Carris network (*Guia*) can also be obtained from the main Metro stations, eg Rotunda and Rossio.

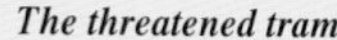

The threatened tram

Lisbon trams

Much has been written about Lisbon's trams in recent years. These wonderful vehicles, some pre-World War I, made in Sheffield, should be an essential part of any holiday. The wooden benches and brass fittings, the nameplates and the special open-window trams have struck a nostalgic chord even with the *lisboetas* themselves. It is no wonder that the authorities, who would like to banish

Line 28

them from the streets, have been inundated with protests. The high seats near the windows provide passengers with a splendid, unobstructed view of the bustling city streets. There is an ever-changing scene as the trams negotiate the steep hills and narrow, twisting streets.

Users should be aware that at the weekends the tram service is either irregular, non-existent or replaced by a bus service. The system for fare collection can vary, depending on whether a conductor is on board or not, but it is more convenient and cheaper to buy a tourist pass or a ticket booklet in advance (*see page 89*).

Line 28 is the most popular route for tourists, as it is a combination of a sightseeing tour and a trip on a roller-coaster. Linking the Basílica da Estrela (*see page 56*) with Praça do Comércio, the cathedral and the edge of the Alfama district, it winds its way along narrow streets before emerging in the Graça quarter (*see page 27*).

Other routes are also worth trying: instead of going by taxi or a train to Belém (*see page 44*), try taking a tram (numbers 15 and 17) from the western end of Praça do Comércio.

Line 24 also takes in some delightful parts of the city and the novelty of the experience will be enhanced by riding in the Elevador de Santa Justa (*see page 28*) to Largo do Carmo, where this route starts. It circles the city in a wide arc, but the journey can be interrupted at any point and a relaxing stroll through the Parque do Príncipe Real is worthwhile.

Elevador de Santa Justa

At Largo do Rato, the tram passes the last arch of the huge aqueduct and the impressive Amoreiras Shopping Centre. It then makes a sharp turn to the east and skirts round the northwest corner of the Parque Eduardo VII. Alight here and work backwards on *Route 6* or else stroll back into the city centre down Avenida da Liberdade. Tram route 24, however, continues on its course round the north-east of the city as far as the river, where it takes a sharp right turn and heads back towards the centre, running alongside the river to the terminus just east of the Praça do Comércio.

Line 25 also follows a circular route starting at Basílica da Estrela. It crosses Largo do Rata and Avenida da Liberdade, then doubles back to the Campo dos Mártires da Pátria. From here take the Lavra funicular railway down to Portas de Santo Antão (*Route 1*) or continue by tram through Baixa and back down to the Basílica.

In the near future some of these tram routes are likely to be replaced by buses. To satisfy the tourists, an old-fashioned tram will be brought back into service and will ply between Belém and Lisbon, no doubt at several times the current fare. As long as the genuine *eléctricos* are still running, they are infinitely preferable whatever the cost.

Facts for the Visitor

Customs and Travel Documents

Residents from Continental European Union countries require an identity card; Britons and others need a passport. They can stay three months before applying for a visa; Canadians and Americans can stay two months. Extension visas can be obtained from the Portugese Embassy before the visit or, once in Lisbon, from the Serviçio de Estrangeiros, Avenida António Augusto de Aguiar 18.

Tourist information map

Tourist information

United Kingdom: Portuguese National Tourist Office, New Bond Street House, 1/5 New Bond Street, London W1Y 0NP, tel: 071 493 3873.

United States of America: Portuguese National Tourist Office, 590 Fifth Avenue, New York, NY 10036-4704, tel: 354 44 003-8.

In Lisbon: The main tourist office for both the city and the country is to be found in the Palácio Foz, Praça dos Restauradores, tel: 346 7031/346 2531. Hotel reservations can also be made here.

Currency

The unit of currency is the escudo ($, sometimes Esc). Coins come in denominations of 1, 2.50, 5, 10, 50, 100 and 200 escudos and there are bank notes of 500, 1,000, 5,000 and 10,000 escudos.

It is generally advisable to change money in Portugal rather than before travelling, but it is now possible to use Eurocheque cards and credit cards in certain cash machines or *caixa automatica*.

Tipping

Restaurants include the cost of service *(serviçio)* in the price, but an additional tip of around 10 percent is always gratefully received. Gratuities are also given to usherettes, hairdressers, taxi drivers and tourist guides.

Opening times

Banks: Monday to Friday 8.30–11.45am, 1–2.30pm.

Shops: There are no strict rules about opening hours. In general, shops are open 9am–1pm and then 3–7pm, while supermarkets stay open all day. In the new shopping centres, many shops open at 10am or even wait until after lunch, but then stay open until 10pm or later.

Museums

Museums sometimes close for renovation work without giving prior notice. Opening times can also change at short notice. Check with tourist offices.

Public holidays

The Portuguese people enjoy four national holidays: 25 April, 10 June, 5 October, 1 December.

In addition, New Year, Good Friday, May Day and 15 August (Assumption Day), 1 November (All Saints' Day), 8 December (Immaculate Conception) and 25 December are also annual holidays. The people of Lisbon honour their patron Santo António on 13 June. Festivities take place the night before, when practically the whole of Lisbon seems to take to the streets.

City post office

Post (Correio)

The main post office is in Praça dos Restauradores 58 and it offers the best service to tourists who have difficulty with the language. It is open from 8am until midnight, while other post offices are usually open from 9am–1pm and 3–6pm.

Calling home

Telephones

Call boxes accept 10, 20 and 50 escudo coins, but for long-distance and international calls a phone card *(credifon)* is recommended. These cards are available from post offices and kiosks. Cheap-rate calls can be made between 8pm and 8am and at the weekend.

Call boxes accept either coins or special charge cards: small ones are worth 50 units, large ones 120 units. Some bars and most hotels have phones where you pay after making the call, but the price of a unit is likely to be double. Coin boxes only take small coins, so an international call is best made at one of the two principal assisted booths: at the main post office (*Correios*) in Praça dos Restauradores, or at the Telefones office in Rossio opposite the National Theatre. Both stay open late, until 10 or 11pm. They get busy at the end of the work day, around 7pm.

International calls: dial 00, then the country's code: 44 for the UK, 1 for the US and Canada, 353 for Ireland, 61 for Australia, 33 for France and 49 for Germany. AT&T 05017-1-288; Sprint 05017-1-877; MCI 05017-1234.

Fax: the larger hotels have fax facilities. Facilities are also advertised in some shops. The Telefones office at the top of Praça Rossio has a fax service.

Newspaper kiosk

Time differences

In 1993 Portugal fell into line with European Union countries. The time in Lisbon is now one hour ahead of Greenwich Mean Time and six hours ahead of Eastern Standard Time. The clocks are changed in March and September.

Entertainment guides

Every Wednesday, the newspaper *Sete* or *Se7e* gives a summary of 'what's on' in the next seven days.

Hairdressers
Men who appreciate a quick and inexpensive wet shave in the morning will find Lisbon well supplied with gentlemen's hairdressers.

Dress
Foreigners are expected to abide by the same standards of dress as the Portuguese themselves. Shorts are generally not acceptable and to wear sandals is considered the same as going barefoot. Visitors to churches and monasteries should always dress appropriately.

Doctors and chemists
In urgent cases, call 115. Otherwise take a taxi to *Urgência*, the accident and emergency ward of a hospital. There are half a dozen large hospitals in the city and a central phone number: 860131/873131.

Chemists (*Farmácias*) are open from 9am to 1pm (including Sunday) and from 3pm to 7pm. When closed, all chemists have a list on their doors highlighting the nearest open chemist.

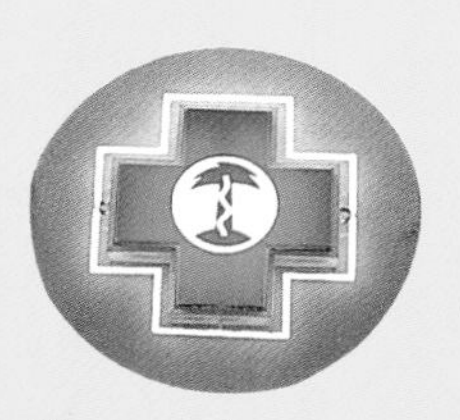

Pharmacy sign

Emergencies
Dial 115 for police and ambulance.

In case of emergency ...

Theft
Petty crime has risen dramatically during the last few years. Take particular care on public transport as some notoriously skilful thieves and pickpockets take advantage of visitors' unfamiliarity with the system and also of the large crowds of people. One undesirable phenomenon is hand-bag snatching by thieves on mopeds. Cars parked near the beach are very vulnerable to thieves and it is inadvisable to leave anything of value in a parked car. Any loss must be notified to the police if an insurance claim is to be made and victims of theft are recommended to use the police station in Rua Capelo in the Chiado district as English-speaking police are on duty there.

Lost property
Contact the nearest police station to collect lost property. The central police lost property office *(Secção dos achados)* has temporarily closed.

Diplomatic representatives
Canada: Rua Rosa Arújo 2, No 6, tel: 56 38 21.
Ireland: Rua da Impresa a Estrela 1, No 4, tel: 66 15 69.
United Kingdom: Rua Spa Domingos à Lapa 37, tel: 3 96 11 91
United States of America: Avenida das Forces Armadas, 16, tel: 7 26 66 00.

Accommodation

Hotels and pensions

Hotel sign

During the summer months Lisbon is one of Portugal's top tourist attractions, with most of the visitors coming from neighbouring Spain. Rooms in hotels in the lower and middle price bands are usually taken by around 6pm on most days. New hotels are under construction at the moment, but they are most likely to be in the high price band. The Palácio Foz information centre in Praça dos Restauradores will help to find rooms, but visitors are strongly recommended to book in advance.

Hotels in Portugal are divided into five categories, while *pensions* are divided into four bands. Four- and five-star hotels are described here as *$$$L*, *$$$* (first-class accommodation), three-star hotels are *$$* (very good quality), and two- and one-star hotels as *$* (good). Rooms in *pensions* correspond generally with the category which is one star lower than the hotel, eg a four-star *pension* is equal to a three-star hotel. *Pensions* with only one star are not recommended. The hotel management in every hotel must display a list of current prices, plus any additional charges such as breakfast, extra bed, etc. Hotels include the price of breakfast in their charges.

Pension sign

Luxury hotel

Tivoli Lisboa Hotel

An indication of likely charges for a double room with bath is as follows:

$$$L	hotels	30,000–60,000 escudos ($)
$$$	hotels	15,000–40,000$
$$	hotels	10,000–20,000$
$	hotels	8,000–10,000$

The following is a small selection of accommodation available in the city:

$$$L **Ritz Inter-Continental**, Rua Rodrigo da Fonseca 88, tel: 69 20 20; **Sheraton**, Rua Latino Coelho 1, tel: 57 57 57; **Tivoli**, Av. da Liberdade 185, tel: 53 01 81.

$$$ **Altis**, Rua Castilho 11, tel: 52 24 96; **Avenida Palace**, Rua 1 de Dezembro 123, tel: 3 46 01 51; **Tivoli Jardim**, Rua J C Machado 7, tel: 53 99 71; **Pensão Residência, York House**, Rua das Janelas Verdes 32, tel: 3 96 25 44. This hotel, formerly a convent, is in an old and interesting quarter, near the Museu Nacional de Arte Antiga and is under English management. Ask for rooms at the rear of the building (noisy traffic); **Die Dependance**, Rua das Janelas Verdes 47, lacks the same charm.

$$ **Eduardo VII**, Av. Fontes Pereiro de Melo 5, tel: 53 01 41; **Miraparque**, Av Sidónio Pais 12, tel: 3 52 42 86 (quiet location); **Roma**, Av. de Roma 33, tel: 76 77 61;

Waiting for the tour coach

Botânico, Rua Mãe de Água 16, tel: 3 42 03 92; **Britânia**, Rua Rodrigues Sampaio 17, tel: 3 15 50 16.

$ **Borges**, Rua Garrett 108–110, tel: 3 46 19 51 (pleasant, peaceful location in the Chiado quarter); **Roma**, Travessa da Glória 22 A, tel: 36 05 57; **Alicante**, Av. Duque de Loulé 20, tel: 53 05 14; **Súiço Atlântico**, Rua da Glória 13–19, tel: 3 46 17 13; **Americano**, Rua 1 de Dezembro 73, tel: 32 75 19 (central location, but noisy).

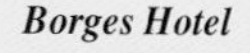

Borges Hotel

Tomar

$$ **Dos Templários**, Largo Cândido dos Reis, tel: 0 49/31 21 21;*$* **União**, (*pension*), Rua Serpa Pinto, tel: 0 49/31 28 31 (simple, but in a central location and quiet).

Évora

(very busy in summer; reservation advisable)

$ **Pousada dos Lóios**, Largo do Conde de Vilar Flor, tel: 0 66/2 40 51; *$$$* **Planície**, Largo Alvaro Velho 40, tel: 0 66/2 40 26; *$* **Santa Clare**, Travessa da Milheira 19, tel: 0 66/2 41 41.

Youth Hostels

Pousada de Juventude, Rua Andrade Corvo 46, tel: 53 26 96 (normally very crowded).

Outside the city but easily reached by train from Cais do Sodré: **Catalazete**, Estrada Marginal, 2780 Oeiras, near Inatel, tel: 4 43 06 28; also **Sintra**, Santa Eufémia, 2710 Sintra.

Camping

Monsanto, Parque Municipal de Campismo de Monsanto (west of the city centre), tel: 70 44 13/70 83 84. Open all year.

Index